A Look at the Sun

Ray Spangenburg and Kit Moser

Franklin Watts

A DIVISION OF SCHOLASTIC INC.
NEW YORK · TORONTO · LONDON · AUCKLAND
SYDNEY · MEXICO CITY · NEW DELHI · HONG KONG
DANBURY, CONNECTICUT

For

NED *and* AMY

Photographs ©: AKG London: 16 (Oris Battaglini), 13 (Erik Bohr), 23; Corbis Sygma/D. Goupy: 8; Corbis-Bettmann: 47 (Roger Ressmeyer/NSO/SEL), 61 (UPI), 15; Liaison Agency, Inc.: 77 (Marc Biggins), 60 (Hulton Getty); Mary Evans Picture Library: 17 (Explorer Archives), 19, 21, 28, 59, 66; NASA : 39, 56, 57, 80 (Solar and Heliospheric Observatory), 88; Photo Researchers, NY: cover, 54 (Julian Baum/SPL), 86, 109 (John Chumack), 52, 62, 70, 104 (ESA/SPL), 82, 83 (Jack Finch/SPL), 14 (François Gohier), 24, 25, 50, 92 (David A. Hardy/SPL), 42, 98 (Jisas/Lockheed/SPL), 12 (Adam Jones), 31 (Jerry Lodriguss), 67 (Mark Marten/Los Alamos National Laboratory), 10 (Del Mulkey), 45 (NASA), 2, 73, 103 (NASA/SPL), 34, 35 (David Parker/SPL), 81 (Jerry Schad), 33 (SPL), 29 (Frank Zullo); Photri: 36, 38, 75, 79, 87, 97, 110; Yerkes Observatory/University of Chicago: 48.

The photograph on the cover shows *SOHO* orbiting the Sun. The photograph of the Sun's outer atmosphere, or corona, shown opposite the title page was captured by the TRACE satellite on May 5, 1998.

Library of Congress Cataloging-in-Publication Data
Spangenburg, Ray.
    A look at the Sun / by Ray Spangenburg and Kit Moser.
        p. cm.—(Out of this world)
    Includes bibliographical references and index.
    ISBN 0-531-11764-2 (lib. bdg.) 0-531-16565-5 (pbk.)
    1. Sun—Juvenile literature. [1. Sun.] I. Moser, Diane, 1944- II. Title.
III. Out of this world (Franklin Watts, Inc.)

QB521.5 .S72 2001   00-051346
523.7—dc21

GROLIER
PUBLISHING

Acknowledgments

We would especially like to thank the many people who have contributed to *A Look at the Sun*. First of all, special appreciation goes to our editor, Melissa Stewart, whose steady flow of creativity, energy, enthusiasm, and dedication have infused this series. We would also like to thank Sam Storch, Lecturer at the American Museum-Hayden Planetarium, who reviewed the manuscript and made many insightful suggestions. Also, to Tony Reichhardt and John Rhea, once our editors at the former *Space World* magazine, thanks for starting us out on the fascinating journey we have taken during our years of writing about space.

Contents

Hovering above the horizon, the Sun paints
intense pink and violet hues across the water,
the sky, and the rocky coast of Brittany, France.

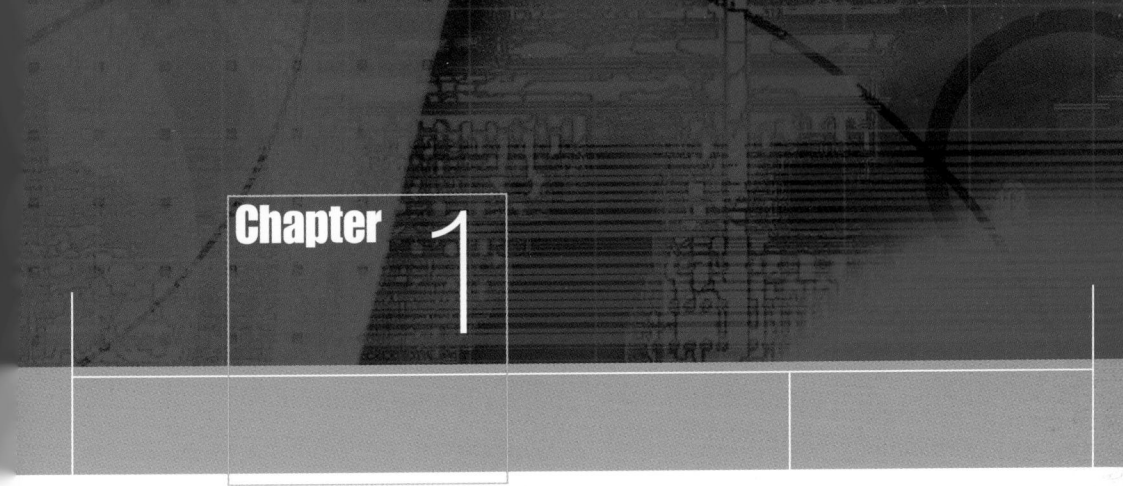

Star of the Solar System

From Earth, the Sun appears as a bright disk in the sky. It is the source of August's broiling heat, but it also warms the land on winter's coldest days. At dusk, the Sun hovers on the horizon, painting the sky with lovely shades of bright pink, yellow, and red. Each dawn, our Sun brings a new day to our lives.

However, there is another way to think about the Sun—as a star. The Sun is 92,955,808 miles (149,597,870 kilometers) from Earth, making it the closest star in the universe. The Sun is part of a galaxy, or group of stars, known as the Milky Way. Like other stars, our Sun is an immense ball of hot, glowing gases.

The Sun is not only the center of the solar system, its pulse radiates out to every object and affects every corner of our neighborhood in space. The Sun's energy reaches out to Earth and billions of miles beyond to the very edges of the solar system.

For humans, the most important of the Sun's far-reaching effects is the energy that bathes Earth and sustains what may be the rarest phenomenon in the universe—life. The Sun provides the warmth, light, and energy that nearly all life on Earth needs to survive. No other object in the sky is so important. Plants require the Sun's rays. Without sunlight, the forests of Alberta, Canada, would not exist. The

The Sun filters through forest branches, bringing life to plants and creatures beneath their umbrella.

grasses on the plains of Kansas would not sprout. The Olympic Peninsula in Washington would be barren. There would be no lush, green covering of mosses, ferns, or tall timber. The tulips and the roses would not bloom. No lettuce, tomatoes, or oranges would grow in California's Central Valley. If the Sun vanished tomorrow, Earth's animals would disappear too. The Sun is necessary for the existence of nearly all life on our planet.

The Sun can also have negative effects on living things. Its *ultraviolet rays* can damage our skin and the protective covering of other creatures—especially in places where the ozone layer in Earth's upper atmosphere is thin. As the Sun's rays strike our home planet, some of their heat energy becomes trapped below Earth's atmosphere and slowly warms the surface.

This process, known as the *greenhouse effect*, works to the advantage of living things—unless something throws off the balance. Then our precious planet may start to overheat, and global warming will occur. Polar ice caps will melt and the sea level will rise. Plants will die or migrate northward. Animals will have to move too. If the warming continues, most of Earth's creatures will eventually die. Venus, with its surface temperatures of 900°F (480°C) is a grim example of the insufferable heat that can result when a greenhouse effect goes out of control.

Without the Sun, though, the complex dynamics that create Earth's weather—the delicate balance among oceans, atmosphere, radiation from the Sun, and other factors—would cease to exist. There would be no changing seasons—no colorful autumn leaves or chilly winter snows, no spring daffodils, and no long summer evenings. The polar ice caps would slowly expand and creep over Earth's entire surface, but no one would be around to worry about it. Without the Sun,

The tilt of Earth's axis and the angling rays of the Sun bring us the changing seasons—from the icy days of winter to summer's hot, steamy afternoons.

humans could not survive. Our home planet, our oasis in space, would be nothing more than a frozen, lifeless rock.

Ancient Views of the Sun

In recognition of the Sun's importance, many early cultures worshiped a Sun god. They knew that the Sun brought light and warmth to their days. They knew that the Sun's relative position throughout the year was linked to the seasons and the cycle of their crops. They often prayed to the Sun god to protect their crops and sought his favor through sacrifices or other rituals.

Each early culture had a different name for its Sun god. The ancient Egyptians called him Amon-Re or Ra. The ancient Greeks believed that, each day, the Sun god Helios drove a horse-drawn chariot from horizon to horizon—representing the Sun's journey across the sky. The Romans called the Sun-god Sol. Roman emperors considered him their prime protector. Ancient people in India, Africa, and Aztec Mexico also worshiped the Sun.

This ancient Greek sculpture shows the god Helios driving his chariot across the sky.

From earliest times, *solar eclipses* had great importance all over the world. Today we know that during a solar eclipse, the shadow of the Moon falls across Earth's surface as the Moon passes in front of the Sun. However, to early humans, the darkened daytime sky must have been truly frightening. As the sky deepened to a slate-blue and became dark enough to show starlight and planets, ancient peoples believed the Sun had disappeared forever. No doubt, they wondered what they had done to anger the gods enough for such an extreme punishment.

In ancient times, people became frightened when the Sun disappeared during a total solar eclipse. Today we know what causes eclipses.

Eventually, early astronomers realized that eclipses were not a sign of their gods' wrath. In fact, they were predictable cosmic events. Some cultures could forecast eclipses months or even years in advance. A classic Chinese story, *Shu Ching*, tells the fate of two court officials, Hsi and Ho, whose job it was to announce heavenly events during the reign of Chung K'ang. Unfortunately, they wined and dined a little too much, forgot to do their job, and failed to warn people about an eclipse that occurred in 2137 B.C. For this oversight, the two men lost their lives.

More than 2,000 years ago, a Greek mathematician named Hipparchus of Nicaea used a solar eclipse to determine the distance from Earth to the Moon. He compared observational data from two sightings of the eclipse—one at Hellespont in what is now Turkey and the other in Alexandria, Egypt. Then he used the surveyor's technique of triangulation to estimate the distance to the Moon.

Ancient astronomers understood the relationships between the Sun's cycles and life on Earth. They could see that the change from long days to shortened peri-

The Greek mathematician Hipparchus used an eclipse of the Sun to calculate the distance between Earth and the Moon.

ods of light affected crops. They paid attention to the way the seasons changed, and they developed a calendar that predicted the Sun's movement and its relationship to changes on Earth. The Sun's presence in the sky was clearly important for life on Earth, and astronomers had the job of predicting its repeating patterns of movement.

Centering on Earth

Although many ancient philosophers in Greece and other cultures believed that Earth moves around the Sun, this idea was overshadowed by the work of Claudius Ptolemaeus, or Ptolemy, an astronomer who lived about 1,900 years ago. Ptolemy claimed that the Sun, the planets, and the stars all move in perfect, harmonious circles around Earth. He even drew detailed charts to show each planet's movements.

Because Ptolemy was so well respected by his peers, he was able to convince other scholars that his theory was correct. It certainly seemed logical. For thousands of years, people had watched the Sun, Moon, planets, and stars cross the sky. They appeared each night in the east, traveled to the west, and then set—only to repeat the same performance the next night. These objects must travel around Earth, observers reasoned. How else could they get back to the eastern horizon?

Ptolemy's ideas also appealed to people's self-centered desire to believe

The Greek astronomer Ptolemy

that the entire universe must be designed around human beings. Even the leaders of the powerful Roman Catholic Church embraced Ptolemy's geocentric, or Earth-centered, view of the universe. His ideas fit nicely with their teachings.

Ptolemy's "perfect" theory wasn't really perfect though. When other astronomers looked up at the night sky, they noticed that some of the things they observed didn't agree with Ptolemy's predictions. His

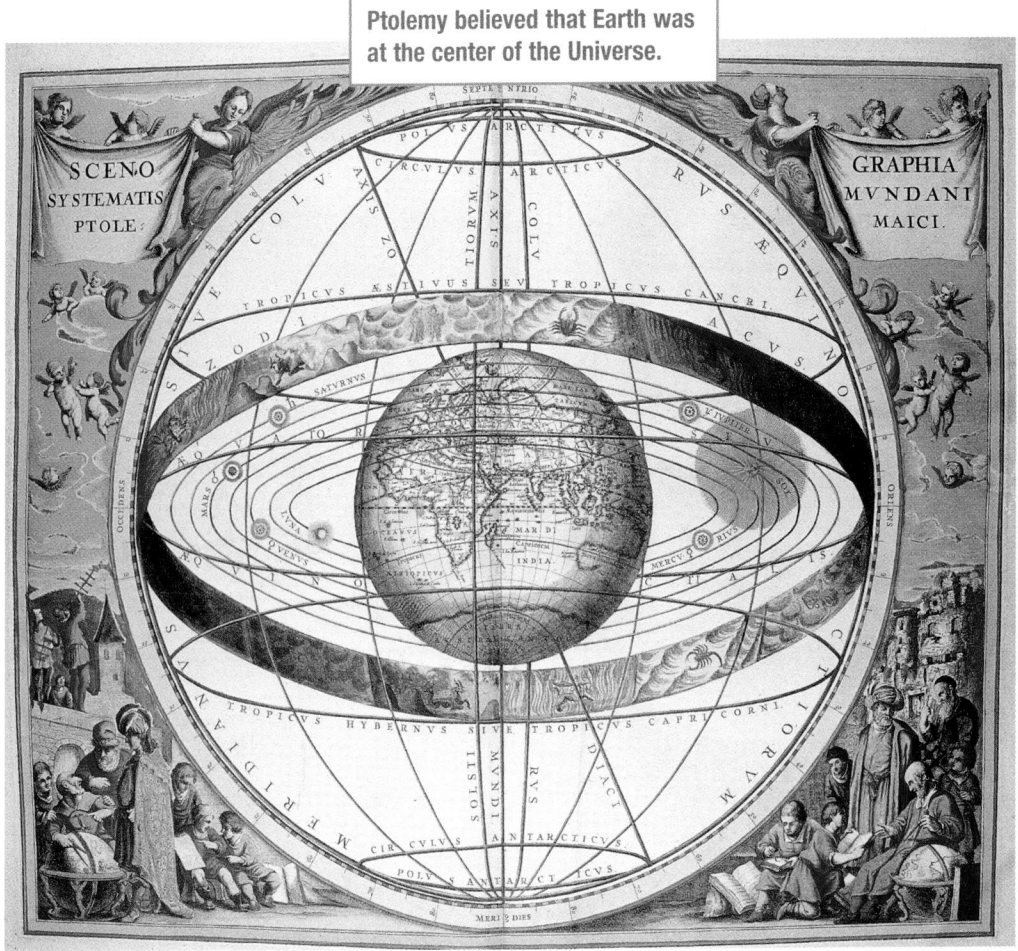

Ptolemy believed that Earth was at the center of the Universe.

star charts didn't always match what was really happening in space. As a result, some people began to question Ptolemy's theory. They thought that perhaps the planets' orbits weren't perfect circles, after all. Despite these doubts, Ptolemy's theory continued to prevail. It was so compelling that people didn't want to abandon it. So scholars began to make minor adjustments to Ptolemy's basic theory to help explain the results of their nightly observations.

The revised system was very complex and awkward, but it appeared to account for the "imperfections" without abandoning the idea that all the planets revolved in perfect circles around Earth. It was a brilliant effort, and it seemed to work. So the geocentric view of the universe continued to be the accepted theory for more than 1,400 years.

Unfortunately, accepted as it was, Ptolemy's theory was completely wrong. Still, hardly anyone questioned it. The power of the human ego was just too great, and the ideals of beauty, perfection, and harmony were too appealing. The Roman Catholic Church's support gave another level of authority to the scientific and philosophical theory, and few people dared to publicly oppose the idea.

No one really challenged Ptolemy's ideas until 1543, when a Polish scholar named Nicolaus Copernicus published a new theory. Copernicus's view of the universe was based on his own observations as well as those made by Greek astronomers thousands of years earlier. Copernicus made careful notations and calculations, and then he developed a theory based on real evidence. Just before he died, Copernicus published his revolutionary idea in a book called *On the Revolutions of the Heavenly Spheres*.

In his book, Copernicus concluded that the Sun—not Earth—is at the center of our solar system. His calculations told him that Earth

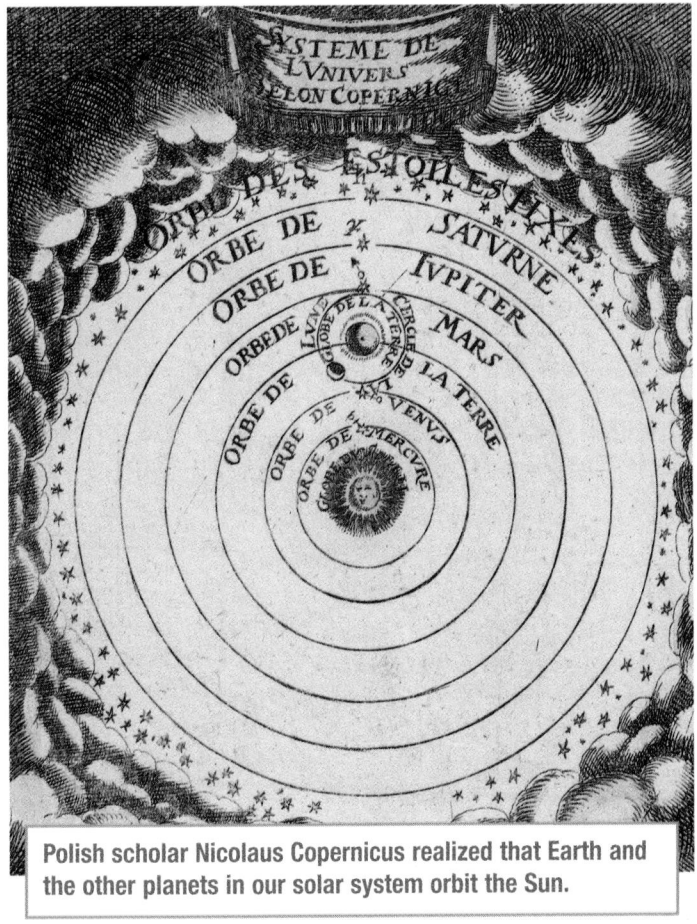

Polish scholar Nicolaus Copernicus realized that Earth and the other planets in our solar system orbit the Sun.

and the other planets orbit the Sun. Earth, he claimed, is not at the center of anything except, perhaps, our human existence.

We now know that Copernicus was right, but his ideas were shocking at the time. However, few people living in the 1500s ever heard about Copernicus's ideas. His work was condemned by religious leaders, and his book was banned. It was not until the 1600s when Copernicus's work was rediscovered and additional proof became available that scholars began to recognize the true structure of our solar system.

Nicolaus's Great Idea

Nicolaus Copernicus was born in Poland in 1473. By the time he was 10 years old, both his parents had died. Nicolaus's uncle, a bishop, became responsible for Nicolaus and his brother. He encouraged both boys to excel in school and attend the University of Krakow.

When Nicolaus was 22 years old, his uncle found him a lifetime appointment as a church official. This meant the young man's income was taken care of for the rest of his life.

Because his church duties were light, Nicolaus had plenty of time to continue his education. He attended several universities, as many students did at the time, wandering like a nomad from one center of learning to another—from Krakow in Poland to Bologna, Padua, and Ferrara in Italy. At these prestigious institutions, he studied medicine, law, and his favorite subject—astronomy.

Nicolaus read everything he could about astronomy and learned about observing the stars and planets. As a critical reader and thinker, he was bothered by the complexities of the geocentric model of the universe. When he returned to Poland, Nicolaus set up a small observatory on the roof above his rooms and began to study the night sky. He also relied on the observations of other astronomers for his own, very careful mathematical calculations. These calculations became the cornerstone of his revolutionary idea that the Sun, not Earth, was at the center of the solar system.

More Sun-Centered Evidence

In the early 1600s, the great Italian astronomer Galileo Galilei (1564–1642) built one of the world's first telescopes and used it to observe the night sky. This important tool allowed him to see many new things. For example, he noticed that the diameter of Mars seemed to vary in size, depending upon when he observed it. He made the same observation about Venus.

Galileo recognized that these variations could only occur if Mars and Venus were much closer to Earth at certain times than they were at other times. Galileo's observations didn't make any sense if the planets circled Earth, but they were exactly what he would expect if the planets revolved around the Sun. Galileo's telescope helped him realize that Copernicus had been right.

In this painting, the great Italian astronomer Galileo Galilei demonstrates one of his telescopes.

The Sun

Vital Statistics

DIAMETER AT THE EQUATOR	864,327 miles (1,391,000 km)
MASS	2.2 thousand trillion trillion tons
DENSITY	1.41
SURFACE TEMPERATURE	9,980 degrees Fahrenheit (5,527 degrees Celsius)
CORE TEMPERATURE	27 million°F (15 million°C)
PERIOD OF ROTATION	At equator: 25.5 Earth-days At the poles: 36.6 Earth-days
AVERAGE DISTANCE FROM EARTH	92,955,808 miles (149,597,870 km)
TIME LIGHT TAKES TO REACH EARTH	8 minutes, 20 seconds
AGE	4.6 billion years
DISTANCE TO THE NEXT NEAREST STAR	4.3 light-years*

* A light-year is the distance light travels in one year, about 5.88 trillion miles (9.46 trillion km).

Galileo communicated these ideas widely, writing and teaching what he had learned. Nevertheless, the Roman Catholic Church still strongly maintained that the planets, Sun, and Moon all revolved around Earth. The Church forbade Galileo to teach his ideas, but Galileo couldn't stop writing and talking about what he knew to be true. In 1633, the Church tried him and sentenced him to house arrest for the rest of his life.

Thanks to Galileo, however, more and more people were beginning to consider a Sun-centered solar system. By the middle of the seventeenth century, most of the world's major astronomers placed the Sun—not Earth—at the center of our solar system. This shift in thinking was very important. It made people understand that Earth moves in the same way as other planets.

The invention of the telescope also enabled scientists to see the planets as disks, like the Moon, rather than just tiny dots of light in the sky. For the first time, people began to think of the planets as "worlds" and the Sun as one of the billions of stars in the universe.

The Birth of Our Star

As astronomers learned more about the Sun and the planets, they began to wonder how our solar system had formed. In 1755, a German physicist and philosopher named Immanuel Kant came up with a possible theory. He suggested that a star and the objects around it form from a giant disk of gas and dust.

At the time, there was no way to prove or disprove Kant's idea. Telescopes were still not powerful enough

German philosopher and physicist Immanuel Kant proposed that a star and the objects that revolve around it begin as a giant disk of gas and dust.

to watch stars as they formed. It was not until more than 200 years later, in the 1980s, that scientists finally developed infrared telescopes that could "see" heat given off by objects in space. With the help of the infrared telescope, astronomers could finally detect infant stars and watch them develop.

Based on infrared telescope observations and other evidence gathered by scientists on Earth and spacecraft that have traveled throughout the solar system, scientists now know that the Sun and the rest of the solar system formed about 4.6 billion years ago.

The Sun began as a huge swirling cloud of hot gas and dust. As the gas and dust particles continuously swirled, a large clump of material began to form at the center of the cloud. As time passed, the cloud contracted and was compressed into a *nebula* shaped like a flattened disk. Although the central clump attracted more and more material, it continued to shrink inward upon itself. The more massive the clump became, the more it contracted and the greater its gravitational pull became. This allowed the clump to attract even more material.

Eventually, the disk became less pancake-like and began to spin more quickly. Now some material remained in orbit around the central clump, instead of getting pulled inward. Some particles were even flung

Scientists believe that the Sun and the rest of the solar system formed from a vast cloud of gas and dust 4.6 billion years ago.

outward toward the edges of the disk, causing an outward flare at its boundaries.

Meanwhile, the central clump of matter, which was made mostly of hydrogen, continued to gain mass, shrink, and heat up. Finally, the pressure at the center of the nebula became so enormous and the heat became so intense that a process called *nuclear fusion* began to take place. When this reaction occurred, hydrogen gas was converted to helium gas, and enormous quantities of energy were released into

space. The massive central clump had essentially become a gigantic hydrogen bomb, and, at that moment, a star was born. That star was our Sun.

The huge disk of hot gases and debris continued to swirl around this infant star. As the orbiting material chilled out, it condensed into larger and smaller masses, including what later became the nine planets, their moons, and the *asteroids* and *comets* that make up our solar system.

Even though scientists now understand how the solar system formed, they continue to have many questions about the Sun. Because the Sun is the closest star to Earth, researchers know it can teach us a great deal about the properties and behaviors of all stars. Over the centuries, researchers have discovered many ways to pry away the Sun's layers, peeling it like an onion so they can take a peek inside—from a safe distance. That effort continues today and will, no doubt, proceed well into the future.

Chapter 2

Exploring the Sun

In 1610, lens making was in its infancy, and telescopes were newly invented—used mostly at sea to spot land or catch sight of approaching ships. When Galileo began using his telescope to observe the skies, he spent some time examining the Sun. Some historians believe that Galileo did not know how much damage the concentrated, focused light could do to his eyes. They claim that viewing the Sun caused Galileo to lose his sight later in life. Other historians disagree. They think that Galileo recognized the potential danger of viewing the Sun directly. According to these experts, Galileo projected the Sun's image through his telescope onto a paper screen—a safe method for observing the Sun and its visible features.

Galileo Galilei was the first person to use a telescope to observe the stars, planets, and other objects in space.

Galileo and other astronomers of his time were the first people to study the dark spots that appear on the surface of the Sun. Galileo noticed that these *sunspots* move around in a predictable pattern. He

Safe Solar Viewing

You should **never** look directly at the Sun—not even through sunglasses or smoked glasses. The Sun's intense light can severely damage your eyes—instantly and permanently. Also, looking at the Sun directly through binoculars or a telescope is never safe—not even when haze or clouds cover the Sun or when the Sun is hidden during a solar eclipse, or when the Sun appears close to the hori-zon at sunrise or sunset. However, you can view the Sun safely by observing its reflected light on a smooth surface. For example, pierce a piece of black paper with a pin, position the pinhole over a mirror, and shine the Sun's reflection on the ground or on the wall of a building. By viewing the reflection, you can take a good, long, safe look at the star of our solar system.

This amateur astronomer is safely observing a partial solar eclipse. She shines the Sun's light through a telescope onto a smooth, flat observation area, where she can see its reflection and the dark shape of the Moon.

was the first person to illustrate this movement by drawing the same sunspots at different times. Based on these observations, Galileo realized that the Sun rotates, or spins, on its axis. Within a few decades, members of the French Academy of Sciences had also figured out the Sun's size and its distance from Earth.

Slowly, popular ideas about the Sun changed. Although the Sun continued to have a very powerful influence on human lives, people no longer thought of it as a god. They now recognized it as an object in our solar system—an object with a diameter more than 100 times greater than Earth's. They realized that the Sun only seems to "rise" and "set." In fact, Earth is moving, not the Sun.

As you stand on our planet's surface, you feel as though you're standing still. Actually, though, you're traveling aboard Earth as it rotates on its axis. One complete rotation takes 24 hours—a day and a night. The cycle you know as a "year" is the time it takes Earth to revolve around, or orbit, the Sun. One complete journey around the Sun takes 365¼ days—or 1 year.

Chasing Eclipses

In the early nineteenth century, the study of the Sun received a boost from an amateur British astronomer named Francis Baily. One of the founders of the British Royal Astronomical Society, Baily had little formal education and spent most of his life as a successful stockbroker. He had always been interested in astronomy, though, and was active in the society throughout his life. In 1825, when Baily was about 51, he was able to retire and turn all his attention to astronomy.

So when a solar eclipse occurred in 1836, he was watching intently. As the last glowing sliver of the Sun disappeared behind the Moon,

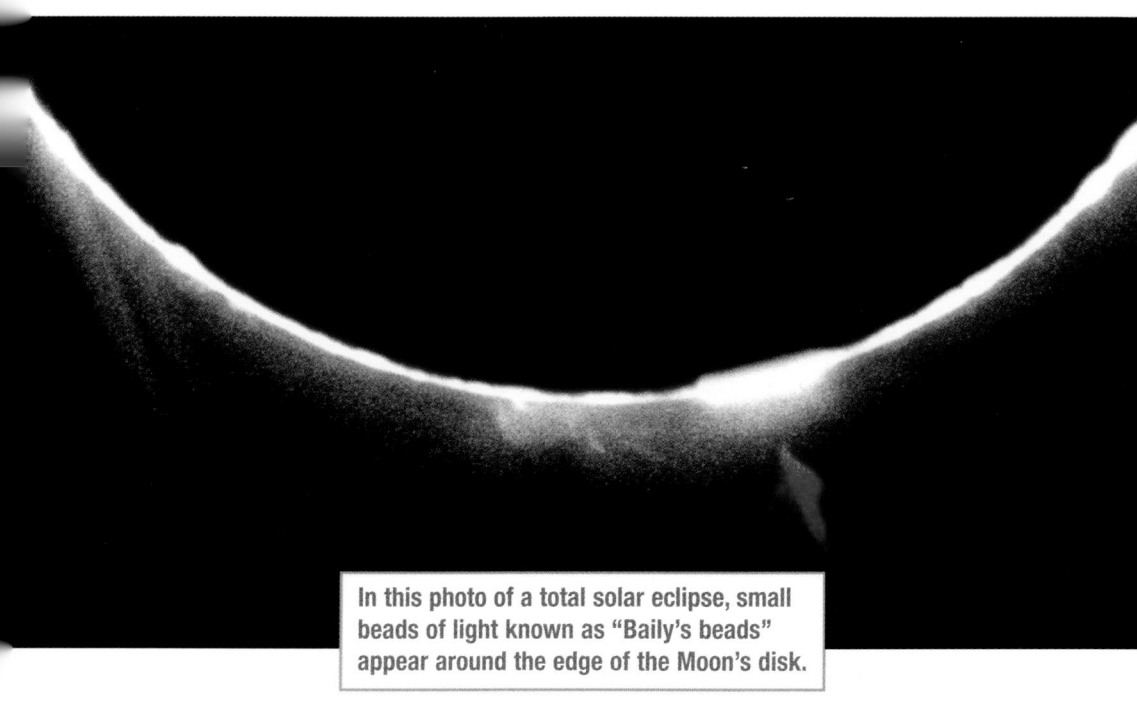

In this photo of a total solar eclipse, small beads of light known as "Baily's beads" appear around the edge of the Moon's disk.

Baily saw something no one else had ever noticed. The light broke up into distinct, bead-like segments, which finally vanished behind the shadow of the Moon. As the Sun reappeared on the other side, the same thing happened—in reverse. As the Sun's light began to peek around the rough edges of the Moon, the very first glimmers of light were not a continuous line. Today, this effect is known as "Baily's beads."

Baily's observation intrigued astronomers all over the world. They began to make plans to view the next solar eclipse from different corners of the world. Soon scientific groups began outfitting teams to observe eclipses from ships in mid-ocean, from high atop mountains, from the equator, and from the tundra of Siberia. The excitement was contagious, capturing the imaginations of amateur stargazers as well as professional astronomers.

The Spectroscope: A Valuable Tool

In the mid-1800s, scientists developed the *spectroscope*—a device that can be used to study the chemical makeup of stars from a distance. When a researcher looks at the white light emitted by a star through a spectroscope, the instrument breaks that light into a spectrum that reveals the elements present in the star.

British scientist Isaac Newton (1642–1727) was the first person to examine the spectrum of visible light in detail. More than a century later, a German optician named Josef von Fraunhofer noticed that sunlight creates a spectrum that contains a number of dark horizontal lines. Fraunhofer was puzzled by the lines. He did not know what they signified. In 1859, a German physicist named Gustav Kirchhoff solved the mystery.

He discovered that chemicals in the upper layers of the Sun absorb some of the Sun's light before it is emitted into space. As light travels from the Sun's hot *core* to the cooler surface, it passes through layers of increasingly cooler gases. This causes the light to bend. When scientists view the spectrum created by the resulting light, each chemical the light has passed through leaves a telltale horizontal line behind. As a result, astronomers can read a spectrum the way a forensic scientist reads a fingerprint.

Working with German chemist Robert Bunsen, Kirchhoff invented the spectroscope to observe and identify the spectra of all the elements known at the time. They even discovered a few elements no one knew about yet.

In 1868, a French astronomer named Pierre Janssen observed strange spectra while viewing a solar eclipse in India. He sent the data to English astronomer Joseph Norman Lockyer, who realized that the

German chemists Gustav Kirchhoff (center) and Robert Bunsen (left) invented spectroscopy. English chemist Sir Henry Roscoe (right) worked with Bunsen on related experiments.

spectra represented a brand new element, which we now call helium. This discovery helped scientists understand the workings of the Sun and other stars.

A star's spectrum has proved to be even more informative than that, though. Spectral lines can also indicate a star's heat source, and the intensities of various lines can provide information about a star's temperature. In addition, scientists have learned to glean clues about the direction of a star's movement and the presence of *magnetic fields* from its spectra.

More Ways to Study the Sun

By the twentieth century, scientists had learned a lot about the Sun by photographing its surface through powerful telescopes. Even today, many kinds of Earth-based telescopes still make important break-throughs in understanding the Sun.

In the past 40 years, though, many other ways to study the Sun have emerged. Beginning in the 1960s, scientists gained two important new tools for studying the Sun—spacecraft and satellites. Astronaut crews aboard the U.S. space station *Skylab* and many Space Shuttle missions have contributed a

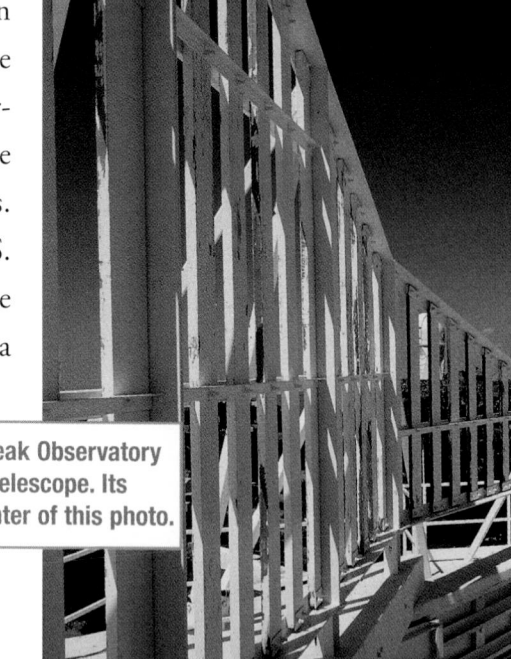

The McMath-Pierce telescope at Kitt Peak Observatory in Arizona is the world's largest solar telescope. Its Sun-tracking mirror appears at the center of this photo.

great deal to our knowledge of the Sun's composition and inner processes. So have an impressive assortment of satellites.

Equipment onboard the *Orbiting Solar Observatories* (*OSO*), which operated from 1962 to 1975, measured *solar flares*, scanned the Sun's surface, recorded fluctuations in the intensity of the Sun's radiation, and studied the *corona*—the Sun's outermost layer.

In 1973 and 1974, astronauts aboard *Skylab* used an X-ray telescope and an ultraviolet *spectroheliograph* to analyze the Sun's composition and capture some 150,000 images of the Sun. Russian cosmonaut crews on the Mir and Salyut space stations also studied the Sun from above Earth's atmosphere.

Between 1980 and 1989, the National Aeronautics and Space Agency (NASA) used a satellite called the *Solar Maximum Mission* (*Solar Max*) to study solar flares. Mission planners originally hoped

that the spacecraft would be able to study the Sun during its most active period, but a technical problem interrupted the mission. In 1984, astronauts aboard the Space Shuttle *Challenger* rescued and repaired the spacecraft. As a result, *Solar Max* was able to collect data for 5 more years.

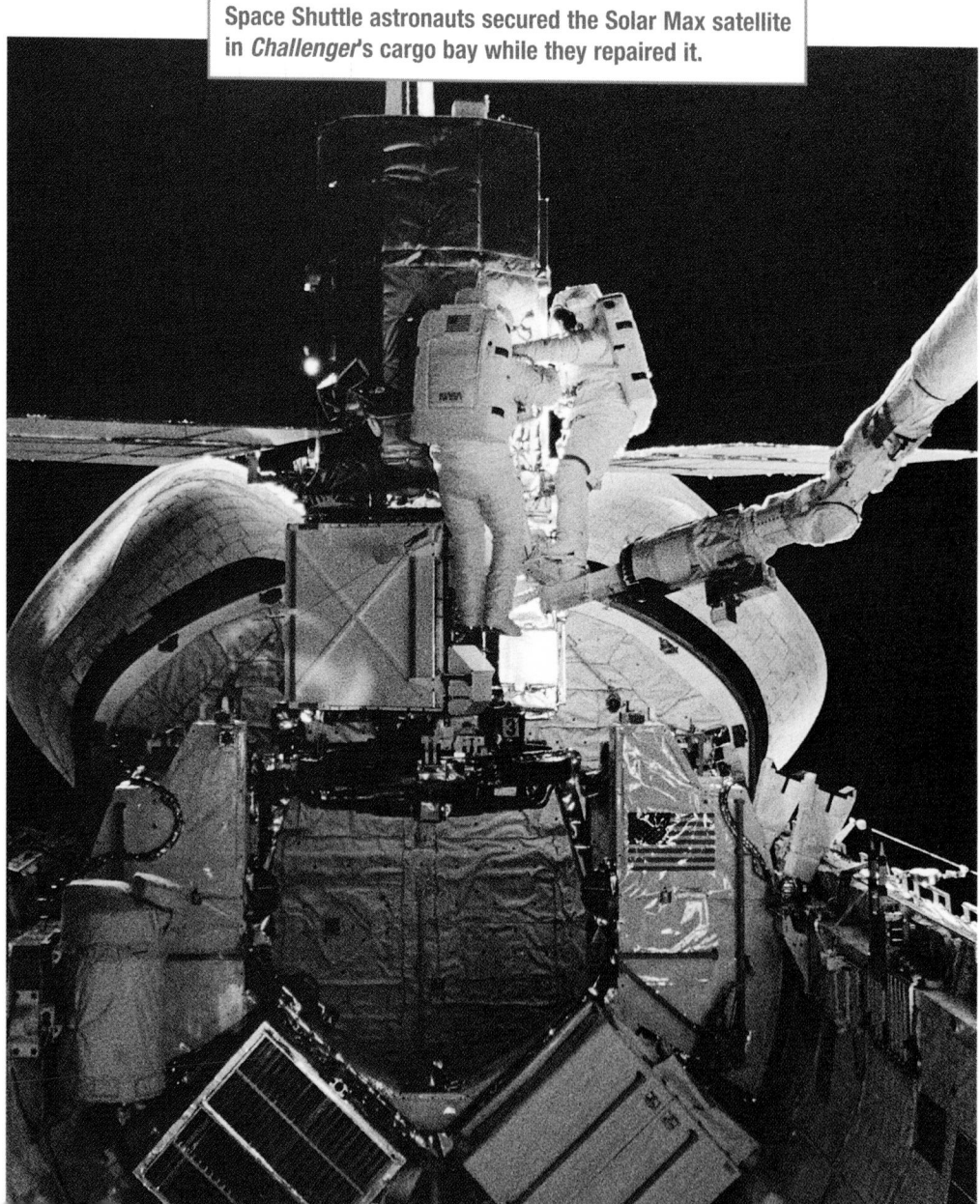

Space Shuttle astronauts secured the Solar Max satellite in *Challenger*'s cargo bay while they repaired it.

Today, scientists consider solar studies to be of the utmost importance to the survival of civilization on our planet. The Sun—our star—also holds the key to scientific understanding of the universe. Solar studies have become an international, cooperative effort.

New Views from *Ulysses*

In 1990, NASA launched a joint NASA/European Space Agency (ESA) spacecraft called *Ulysses* from the Space Shuttle *Discovery*. Once it reached Earth orbit, the spacecraft turned on its booster rockets and started on its way to a special orbit around the Sun—a path that would loop the spacecraft over the Sun's poles. This unusual orbit gave scientists a chance to survey areas of the Sun that they had never seen before.

Engineers knew that getting *Ulysses* to this special polar orbit was going to require some extra energy because the spacecraft would have to leave the orbital plane—the region through which the planets move around the Sun. In the fastest spacecraft launch ever, the 816-pound (370-kg) vehicle traveled at a speed of 7 miles (11 km) per second as it escaped Earth's gravity.

First, *Ulysses* headed for Jupiter—which sounds like the wrong direction! However, by looping past Jupiter, the spacecraft was able to gain an extra boost of speed, known as a *"gravity assist."* While in Jupiter's neighborhood, *Ulysses* studied the planet's magnetism and radiation. Then it sped on to begin its tour around the polar regions of the Sun.

As *Ulysses* swung by Jupiter, the spacecraft used the giant planet's *gravitational field* to pump up its energy and help it speed up and loop out of the orbital plane. Finally, *Ulysses* settled into an orbit that would

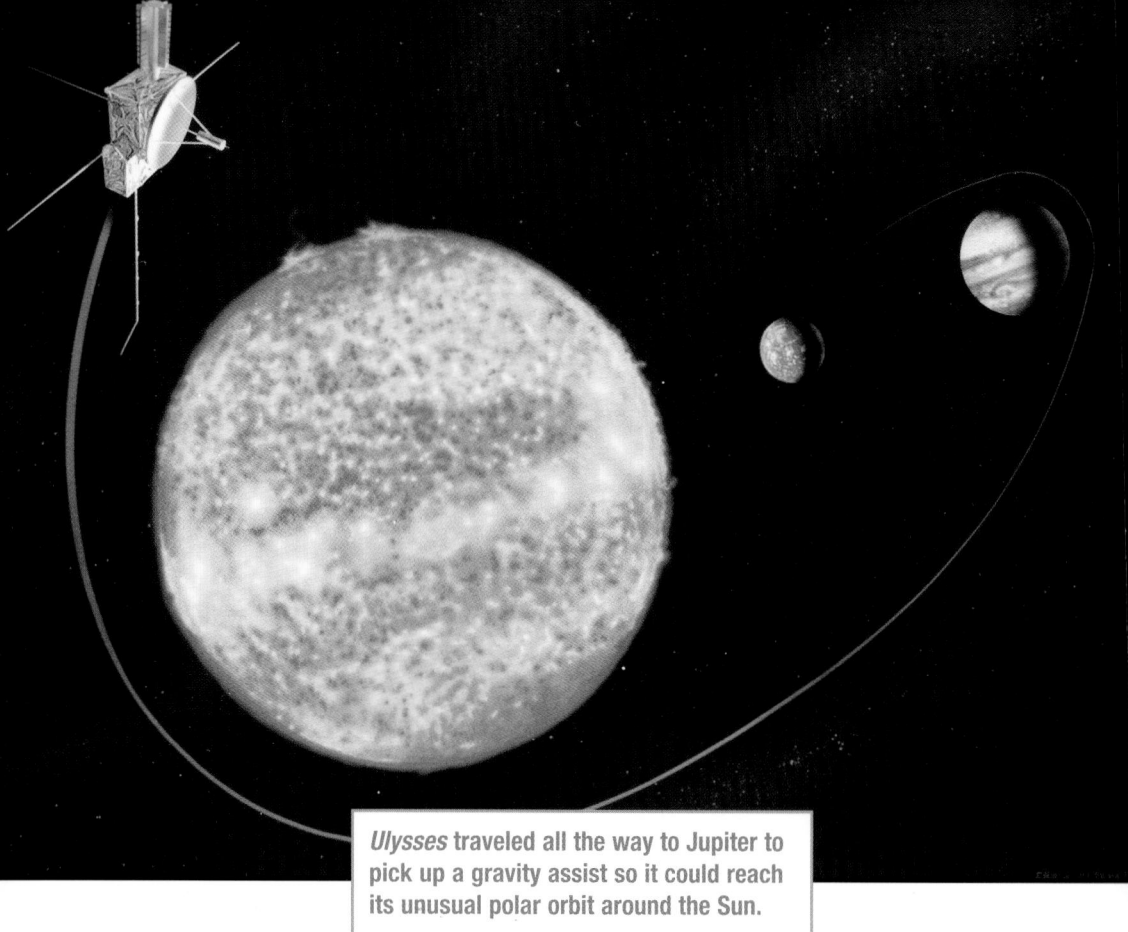

Ulysses traveled all the way to Jupiter to pick up a gravity assist so it could reach its unusual polar orbit around the Sun.

take it above the Sun's poles. The spacecraft began its first pass over the Sun's south pole in the summer of 1994 and zoomed over the north pole in 1995. Then it began its second orbit of the mighty star. The little spacecraft's next close encounter with the Sun came in 2001.

At its most distant point from the Sun, *Ulysses* is more than five times farther from the Sun than Earth is. Strangely, even its closest approach is farther from the Sun than Earth's orbit. Even though *Ulysses* is studying the Sun from a point in space that is always farther away from the Sun than Earth is, the spacecraft has provided a great deal of important information because it has a unique perspective. *Ulysses* carries a lot of equipment for onboard experiments to gain a better understanding of *solar wind*, magnetic fields and particles, interplanetary dust and gas, the corona, and cosmic rays.

More Solar Spacecraft

Another capable observer was the *Yohkoh* solar probe. It was launched in 1991 by Japan, the United States, and Great Britain to study high-energy radiation from solar flares. The X-ray instrument on board helped scientists gain a new understanding of the constant change and violence that takes place within the Sun.

On December 2, 1995, NASA launched another joint NASA/ESA mission to the Sun. This one, the *Solar and Heliospheric Observatory (SOHO)*, set out to study the Sun's internal structure. It was launched

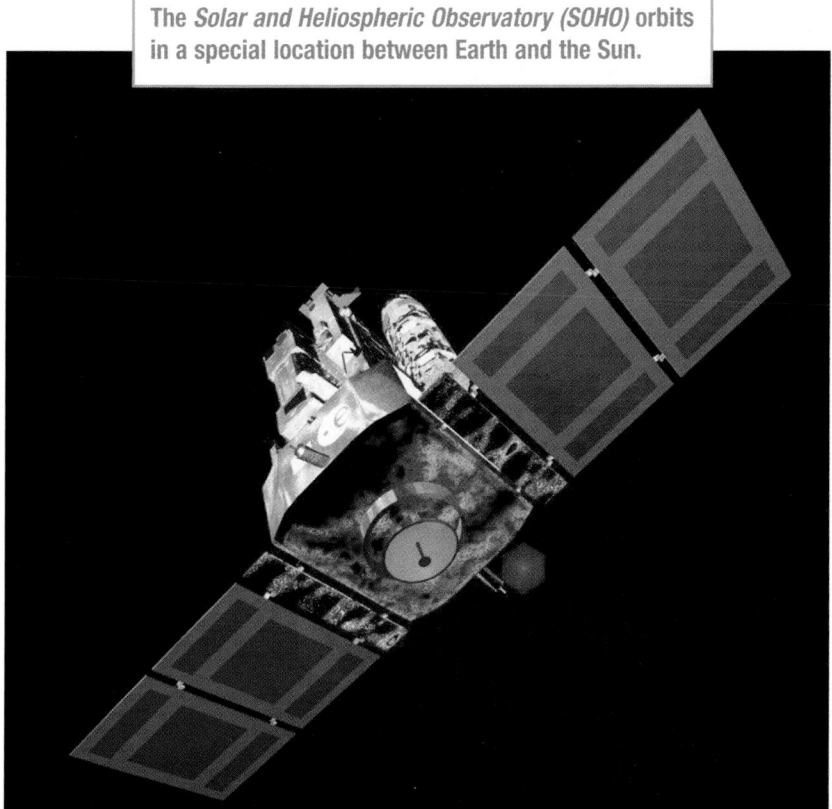

The *Solar and Heliospheric Observatory (SOHO)* orbits in a special location between Earth and the Sun.

into what is known as a "halo orbit," 932,057 miles (1,491,291 km) closer to the Sun than Earth. *SOHO* is positioned at the point where Earth's gravitational pull is balanced by the Sun's gravity, giving astronomers a continuously clear view of the Sun. *SOHO's* powerful instruments monitor the Sun around the clock. They have provided "solar weather updates" and are currently studying the Sun's corona and inner layers.

In 1997, the United States placed the *Advanced Composition Explorer* (*ACE*) spacecraft in orbit to observe the solar wind, the Sun, and the galaxies beyond. It orbits about 932,000 miles (1,499,000 km) from Earth.

In 1998, another spacecraft, the *Transition Region and Coronal Explorer* (*TRACE*), was launched by the United States for an extended mission to study the Sun's upper atmosphere. Like the many spacecraft that came before it, *TRACE* will help scientists gain a better understanding of our favorite star—the Sun.

Chapter 3

The Magnificent Solar Show

In the twentieth century, thanks to observatories in space and on Earth, astronomers discovered that a variety of breathtaking displays of power and brilliance take place on the Sun. These include close-up views of the sunspots first observed by Galileo almost 400 years ago as well as many other solar spectacles that can only be seen with the help of advanced technology.

The Sun, scientists have learned, produces a display of brilliant flashes, enormous explosions, and huge belchings of hot, glowing gases that leap far out into space. All these magnificent shows have one thing in common. They are closely related to the activity of the Sun's powerful magnetic field.

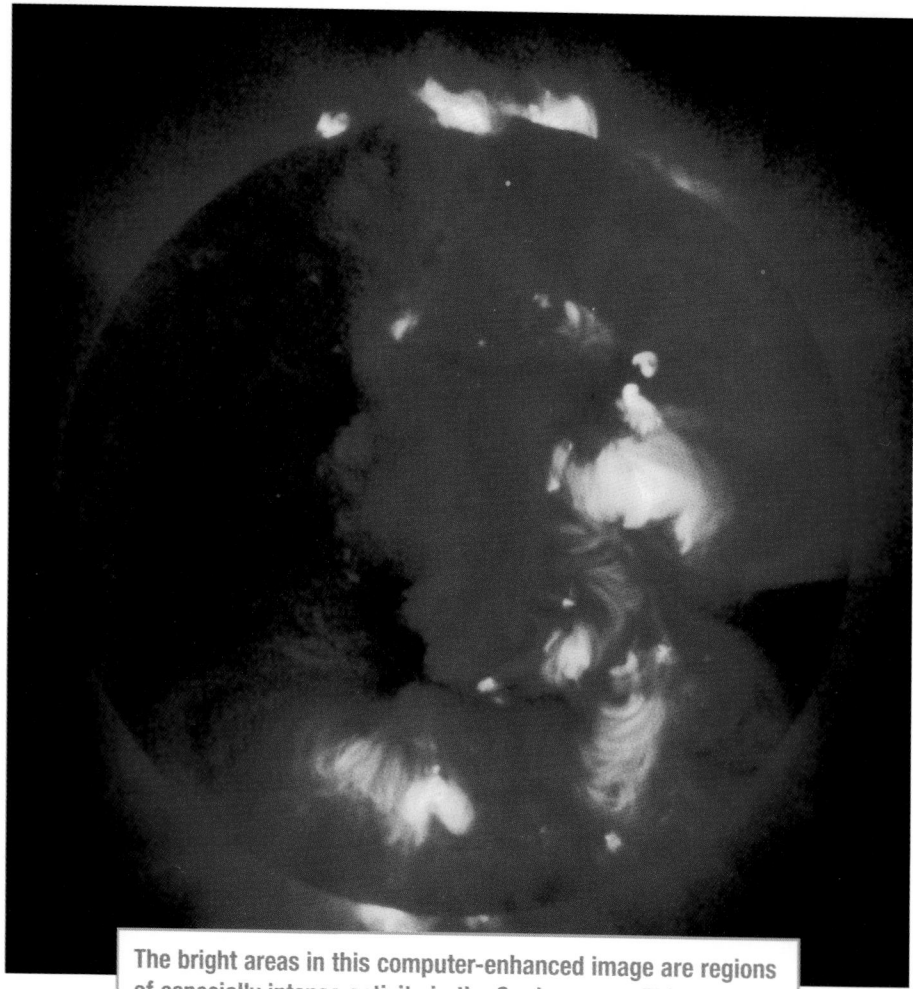

The bright areas in this computer-enhanced image are regions of especially intense activity in the Sun's corona. This image was taken by the Japanese satellite *Yohkoh* in 1991.

Understanding Magnetism

You've probably seen magnets holding paper notes or photos to the steel door of a refrigerator. You may have also seen magnetic advertising signs that cling to the steel doors of some cars and trucks. These objects have been specially designed to produce magnetism, but magnets also exist in nature. The first natural magnets were discovered by the early Greeks and the ancient Chinese. They were rocks, known as lodestones, that attracted metal objects.

It didn't take long for people to realize that when they rubbed a steel needle across a lodestone, the needle became magnetic too. Around 1,000 years ago, the Chinese discovered that when they suspended a magnetic needle, one end always pointed north. That discovery led to the development of a very important invention—the compass. This exciting new navigational device soon became popular among sailors all over the world.

Around 1600, a British scientist and physician named William Gilbert came up with an explanation for why magnetic needles point north: Earth is a giant magnet. More recently, scientists have learned that the Sun is an even bigger magnet. Both bodies have north and south poles and a magnetic field that influences surrounding regions.

In the nineteenth century, British physicist Michael Faraday came up with the idea that magnetism travels along what he called "lines of force." Today the term *magnetic field lines* is more commonly used to describe the same phenomenon. Many physicists of Faraday's time were skeptical about his ideas. They doubted that magnetic fields and magnetic field lines exist. In answer to his critics, Faraday designed a simple experiment to show the patterns of a magnetic field.

You can try this experiment yourself. You'll need a strong bar magnet, a piece of paper, and a handful of iron filings. Place the bar magnet on a table and sprinkle the iron filings on the paper. Then place the paper on top of the magnet and tap the paper. As if by magic—but actually by obeying the laws of physics—the filings rearrange themselves. Clusters of filings collect around the poles at each end of the bar

Every object in the universe that has mass and takes up space is known as *matter*. The book you're holding in your hand is matter. In fact, your hand is also matter, and so is your entire body. The chair you're sitting on is matter, and so is the air you're breathing. Even if you cannot see the air, it is matter because it takes up space. When you blow up a balloon, you can see that air takes up space.

The ancient Greeks were the first people to suggest that matter might be made up of many small particles they called "atoms." For a long time, people believed that atoms were the absolute smallest particles that make up matter. Today we know that atoms are actually made of even smaller particles—electrons, protons, and neutrons. We also know that protons and neutrons are composed of still smaller subatomic particles, known as quarks.

All three atomic particles are extremely small, but compared to electrons, protons and neutrons are large and heavy. Protons and neutrons reside within the *nucleus*, or center, of an atom. Protons have a positive electrical charge, while neutrons are neutral—they have no electrical charge. Electrons are in constant motion outside the nucleus and have a negative electrical charge.

Different combinations of these three particles result in different kinds of atoms. Hydrogen is the simplest atom. It is composed of one proton and one electron. (Hydrogen is the only element that has no neutrons.) Some atoms are composed of dozens of protons, neutrons, and electrons.

All atoms are electrically neutral. They contain the same number of protons and electrons. However, any electrically neutral atom can be changed into an ion. An *ion* is an electrically charged particle. It can be either positive or negative. If an electron is removed, or stripped, from an atom, the balance between electrons and protons is thrown off, creating an ion with a positive charge. If there are more electrons than protons, a negative ion is created.

magnet. The rest of the filings arrange themselves in lines that loop in half-circles from pole to pole. The midpoint in each half circle has fewer filings. The iron filings line up along the magnetic field lines generated by the magnet.

Faraday also discovered that a current of electricity can create a magnet. Electricity is a stream of tiny charged particles called ions. Ions tend to travel along magnetic field lines, almost like beads sliding along a wire.

Inside the Sun, the movement of ions and the force of magnetic field lines can cause some amazing effects. Many of the outbursts and displays related to the Sun's magnetism are not completely understood. They have become the subject of enormous curiosity and many intriguing studies. Among the shows the Sun's magnetic field puts on, scientists have studied—and continue to study—sunspots, solar flares, solar prominences, and *coronal mass ejections.*

Sunspots and Solar Activity

When Galileo Galilei and his contemporaries turned their telescopes toward the Sun in the early 1600s, they noticed dark spots moving horizontally across the face of the Sun. However, no one discovered much else about sunspots for nearly 250 years. Between 1826 and 1843, a

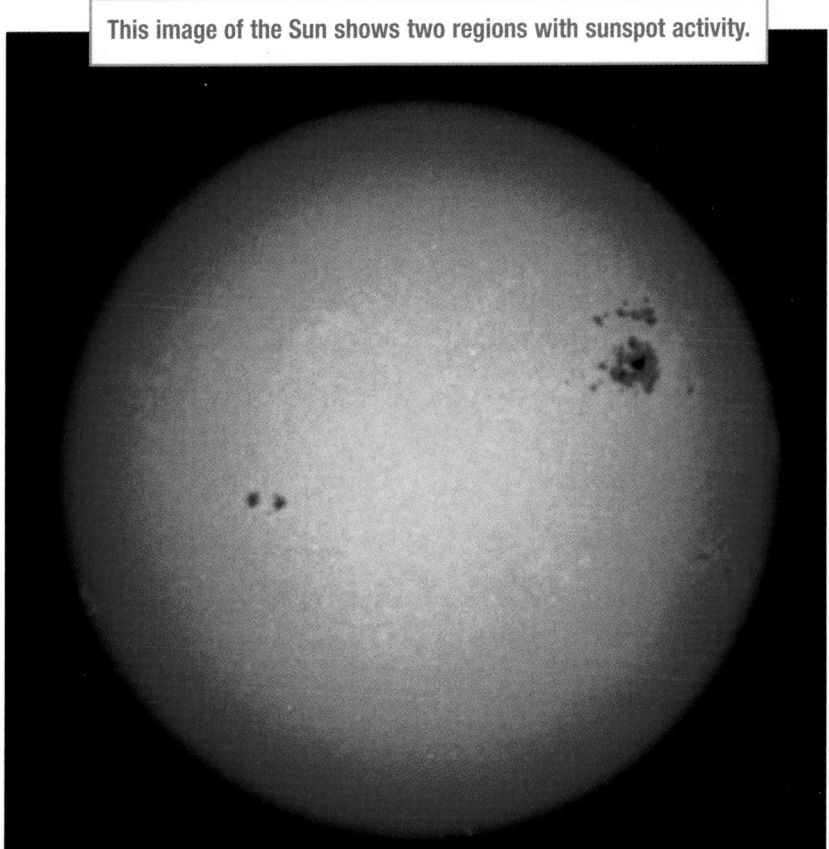

This image of the Sun shows two regions with sunspot activity.

German apothecary named Heinrich Schwabe satisfied his love for astronomy by making careful observations of sunspots. Based on his records, Schwabe realized that sunspots follow a predictable cycle of activity. The Sun's surface alternates between periods of high activity—with lots of sunspots—and periods of low activity when fewer sunspots appear. We now know this activity cycle is about 11 years long.

At the beginning of the cycle, just a few sunspots appear. Some are located about halfway between the equator and the north pole, while others appear halfway between the equator and the south pole. Within a couple of years, the sunspots move closer to the equator and more appear. About halfway through the 11-year cycle, as many as 100 sunspots may appear at one time, almost all near the equator. This stage in the sunspot cycle is known as the solar maximum. For the next few years, the number of spots dwindles, until finally, only a few are visible, still fairly close to the equator. At the same time, a new 11-year cycle begins with a few new spots appearing halfway between the equator and each of the poles.

Close-up images of sunspots reveal that they are not just round, dark spots. Like craters, they dip down below the Sun's "surface," or *photosphere*. Each spot consists of a dark area in the center, called the *umbra*, surrounded by a lighter crown, called the *penumbra*. Dark rays stretch up through the penumbra into the bright photosphere. Sunspot umbras may be up to 11,000 miles (18,000 km) across, and many are large enough to swallow up one or more objects the size of Earth. Compared to the surrounding photosphere, which has an average temperature of about 9,980°F (5,527°C), a sunspot is cool—about 6,200°F (3,427°C). This relative coolness makes a sunspot appear dark next to the brightness of the surrounding photosphere.

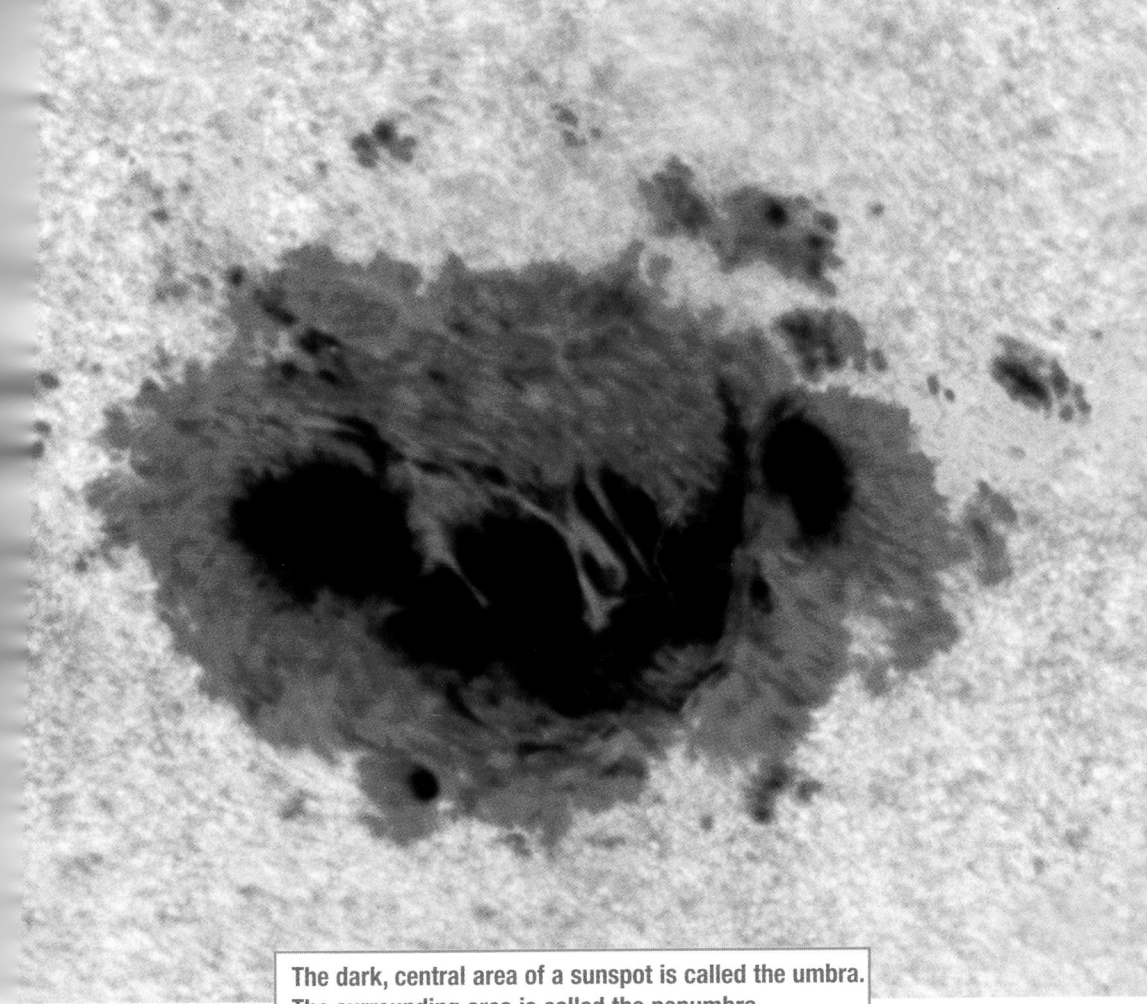

The dark, central area of a sunspot is called the umbra. The surrounding area is called the penumbra.

Individual sunspots may last several days or many weeks, and they often appear in clusters. As Galileo discovered, by watching sunspots we can see the Sun's rotation. By observing them closely, scientists have learned that not all parts of the Sun rotate at the same rate. The gases at the Sun's poles take 30 days to make the trip, while the journey takes only 25 days at the equator.

No one knew what caused these strange, dark areas on the Sun's surface until George Ellery Hale uncovered the first clues in 1908. He found that sunspots have strong magnetic fields. Since then, scientists

Shaker and Mover: George Ellery Hale

One of the greatest forces for the growth of solar astronomy was George Ellery Hale, the founder of solar observational astronomy in the United States. Even as a boy, Hale had a keen interest in science and recognized that doing excellent scientific work was far easier when excellent scientific equipment was available.

While he was still a student at Massachusetts Institute of Technology, Hale invented an instrument called the spec-

George Ellery Hale was a driving force behind the growth of observational astronomy in the early twentieth century.

troheliograph. This device allowed him to photograph the Sun in various spectral wavelengths. He used it to produce some of the earliest images of explosive displays known as *solar prominences*.

In 1892, Hale accepted a position at the University of Chicago on the condition that the school build an observatory. He obtained funding for the entire project from a transportation entrepreneur named Charles T. Yerkes, and the Yerkes Observatory was built in nearby Wisconsin. From then on, Hale spent most of his life observing the Sun and stars, raising money to build better facilities and equipment, and managing observatories.

Hale seemed to have a talent for everything his life touched. He built, organized, and managed major observational institutions with great success. In addition to the Yerkes Observatory, he built the Mount Wilson and Palomar Observatories in California.

At the same time, Hale made some important scientific discoveries. For example, in 1908, he detected magnetic fields within sunspots. Before Hale's discovery, scientists thought magnetic fields existed only on Earth.

Hale also founded two scientific journals for and by professional astronomers, and he organized a project to build one of the largest telescopes in the world. Today, nearly 100 years later, Hale's observatories continue to foster breakthroughs in astronomy as they have done ever since they were founded.

have begun to work out some of the processes that cause these strange holes in the photosphere.

Now that astronomers have mapped the Sun's entire magnetic field, they know that powerful magnetic loops connect one sunspot to another. A typical group of sunspots begins when a magnetic field's lines of force rise up from within the Sun's interior and travel through the photosphere. The group begins with a few small spots. They move apart and grow larger. Over the next few weeks, small spots may disappear, but larger spots often remain longer. Each sunspot has magnetic polarity—either north or south—and the looping magnetic fields usually connect two sunspots with opposite polarities. Something about this process seems to cool the region.

Further research has shown that the sunspot cycle is actually 22 years long—if you take into account a change in magnetic polarity that the Sun and its sunspots undergo. In the Sun's northern hemisphere, the sunspot that leads a group in rotation shares the same polarity as the north pole. In the Sun's southern hemisphere, the setup is the opposite—the south pole and the leading sunspot have the same polarity. Once every 11 years, these polarities reverse. Then the poles have the opposite polarity and so do the leading sunspots in each hemisphere.

Scientists have been studying this cycle for a relatively short time, though, and they still have a lot to learn about sunspots and their patterns. Looking back through historical and physical records, scientists have discovered that the regular 11-year cycle apparently halted between 1645 and 1715. Even though many people now think of sunspots as the source of magnetic storms and unpleasant "solar weather," a lack of sunspots seems to have been a disaster for life on Earth.

Layers of the Sun: A Quick Look

Like a wedding cake, the Sun is made up of many layers. As you have just learned, sunspots form in a layer known as the photosphere. Scientists often think of the photosphere as the "surface" of the Sun. It is the uppermost layer that we can see.

Above the photosphere, float two layers of thin invisible gases—the *chromosphere* and the corona. When you gaze at the Sun, you look straight through these gases—just as you look through Earth's atmosphere on a clear night. The word "atmosphere," like "surface," is a term borrowed from other worlds, and it may be better suited to the rocky planets of the solar system than the Sun.

Below the photosphere lie the *convective zone*, the *radiative zone*, and finally the central core. Heat radiates from the core and slowly travels through the radiative zone to the convective zone. The gases there slowly churn as they are warmed by heat from below, forced upward, cooled as they approach the Sun's surface, and then fall back toward the Sun's center. Eventually the heat reaches the photosphere and is released into the Sun's "atmosphere."

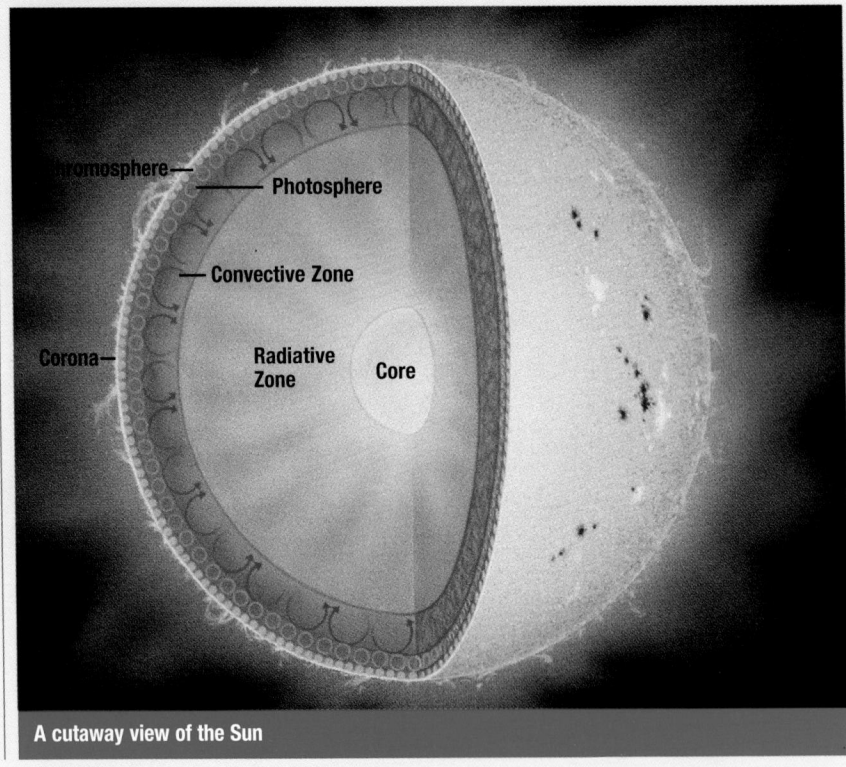

A cutaway view of the Sun

During this period, tree rings and other records show that the weather on our planet was unusually cold. People starved in Europe because they could not raise crops and their animals died from cold or starvation. The Thames River in London, England, froze over—an event that rarely happened before and has never happened since.

Known as the "Little Ice Age," or the Maunder minimum (after E. Walter Maunder, who studied the evidence), this unusually cold weather may have been linked only coincidentally with the lack of sunspots. However, many researchers think this 70-year span of European history shows evidence of a little-understood cause-and-effect relationship between an ice age on Earth and spots on the surface of the Sun.

Solar Flares

A solar flare is a sudden, rapid, and intense release of energy from a localized region of the Sun. This explosive energy is released in the form of *electromagnetic radiation*, energetic particles, and movement of gases. Typically, we see solar flares as bright bursts of light coming from the upper corona—the top layer of the Sun's "atmosphere." Solar flares release enormous amounts of energy and may also give off huge quantities of gases. Temperatures in the area surrounding a solar flare rival the immense heat of the Sun's core.

In a matter of seconds, the explosion accompanying a solar flare can release as much energy as 1 billion 1-megaton thermonuclear explosions. If you could harness the energy of just one solar flare, it would provide enough electricity to power everything that anyone on Earth might need for millions of years.

Solar flares usually occur high above an active group of sunspots, but no one knows why. Some scientists have suggested that the magnetic fields that loop between sunspot umbras may become tangled, twisted, and crowded, causing magnetic field lines to behave like twisted rubber bands. As these lines intertwine more tightly, tension builds. Then, finally, something snaps, and a huge quantity of energy is released in the form of a giant electrical spark accompanied by an enormous explosion. So, sunspots may be closely related to—and may even cause—solar flares.

Studying solar flares helps scientists understand the Sun and its processes better, but these bright, explosive bursts also provide

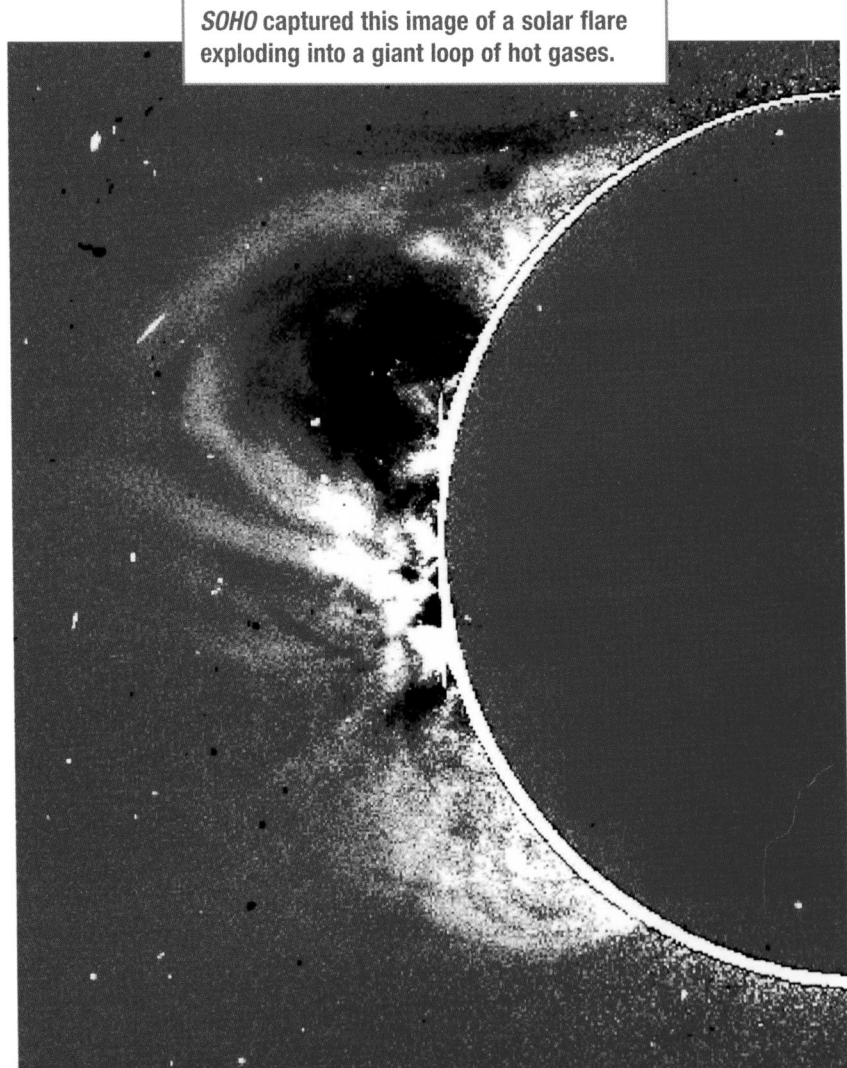

SOHO captured this image of a solar flare exploding into a giant loop of hot gases.

researchers with a better understanding of the processes that go on in other objects in the universe. Among those are flare stars, pulsars, quasars, and black holes. Flare stars are a class of stars that show occasional, sudden, and unpredicted increases in light—much like solar flares but on a much grander scale. Pulsars are burnt-out stars, known as neutron stars, that send out radio waves that pulse on and off. Quasars are far-off objects that resemble faint blue stars and sometimes flare, like flare stars and the Sun. Scientists think quasars may be the centers of an unusual type of galaxy. Black holes are regions in space that have so much mass that even light cannot escape from them.

Solar Prominences

Sometimes, masses of ionized gas—gas composed of charged particles—burst into the corona from below, often looping or double-looping back on themselves. Then these electrical charges come into contact with the corona's own ionized gases. At the same time, the magnetic fields of underlying sunspots attract the charged particles like magnets attract iron filings. Scientists believe that all this movement of ionized particles along the Sun's magnetic field lines may cause one of the Sun's most spectacular displays—the huge clouds of rose, pink, or orange gas called solar prominences.

These light shows take many forms. Sometimes gases break loose and catapult away from the Sun with a dramatic burst of energy. Astronomers call this energy burst an "eruptive prominence." These prominences can travel hundreds of miles from the photosphere through the chromosphere to the corona in as little as an hour. Sometimes an eruptive prominence twists dramatically into a huge figure eight, indicating that a complex magnetic field threads through these

In the background, a loop-shaped solar prominence erupts from the surface of the Sun. In the foreground, a sunspot is visible.

solar particles. If the gases are moving fast enough, they may break away from the Sun's gravity and burst violently into space. However, if the gases are moving a little slower, they may fall back toward the Sun's interior, following the lines of the Sun's magnetic field. When this happens, a kind of "coronal rain" develops.

Another type of prominence, known as a "quiescent prominence," is less spectacular. It occurs when the Sun's magnetic field traps a huge cloud of solar gas high above the Sun's surface, just as the magnetic field around a bar magnet forces iron filings to form a half-circle pattern. This type of solar prominence may stay in place for several hours or even several days. Its arch may be so huge that our entire planet could fit between its lower edge and the surface of the Sun below.

No one completely understands how solar prominences form, but scientists are certain that magnetic fields are involved. Some researchers think the Sun's rotation causes virtually all the activity that takes place on the Sun. The spinning Sun is composed of ionized gas, and the spinning—together with the churning activity of the Sun's convective zone—apparently creates the Sun's magnetism. Because the convective zone is active and makes up about one-third of the Sun's volume, this explanation seems especially likely.

Coronal Mass Ejections

Sometimes the Sun ejects huge bubbles of gas that pass along magnetic field lines. These bubbles are called coronal mass ejections (CMEs). CMEs were first observed between 1971 and 1973 by a spacecraft called the *Seventh Orbiting Solar Observatory* (*OSO 7*). The spacecraft captured many clear, detailed images of CMEs, which may occur as often as several times in a day. These spectacular displays occur when

In 1999, *SOHO* took this image of a coronal mass ejection as it leaps away from the Sun at a speed of about 410,000 miles (650,000 km) per hour. (The disk in the center of the image blocks out the direct light from the Sun to make the corona visible.)

plasma—highly ionized gas—that is usually held in place by the Sun's magnetic field lines suddenly breaks free and bursts into space. CME disruptions can be enormous. When their particles of ionized atoms strike Earth's surface and atmosphere, they often cause damage to power stations and satellites.

CMEs are also responsible for a beautiful display known as an *aurora*. This incredible light show occurs when an enormous quantity of coronal gas is flung into space during a coronal mass ejection. When this happens, a cosmic shock wave reverberates through the solar wind and speeds through space. About 2 days later, it slams into Earth's *magnetosphere*—a vast region of charged particles that surrounds Earth and extends millions of miles toward the outer solar system. The rings of magnetic current that normally encircle Earth's poles receive a massive jolt as a result, and ions form in our planet's upper atmosphere. When a CME arrives, it creates havoc as well as some of the most beautiful light shows in the universe.

Chapter 4

Nuclear Powerhouse

The heartbeat of the Sun begins at its core. The intense heat of the Sun's interior is almost beyond imagination. Gas particles in these regions are compressed so tightly by the weight of particles above them that nuclear fusion continuously converts hydrogen to helium and, in the process, releases enormous quantities of energy, which push outward from the core. Nuclear fusion is the source of all the energy the Sun produces, and it drives all the other reactions that take place in the Sun's many layers of gases. It even powers many of the violent eruptions at the Sun's surface.

An Early Theory

In the 1860s, two physicists, William Thomson, Baron Kelvin of Largs, and Hermann von Helmholtz, first explored some important questions

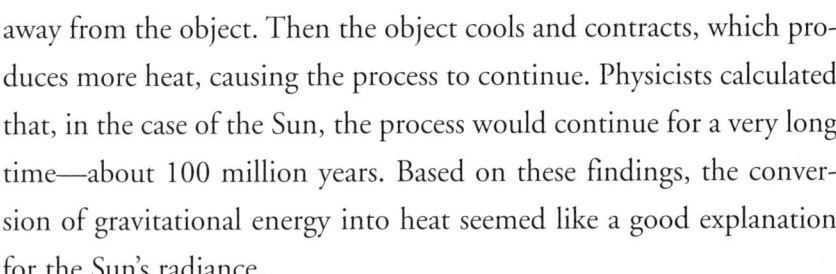

about what goes on deep inside the Sun. The two scientists soon realized that the gravity holding the Sun's mass together must create an immense squeeze within the Sun. They surmised that the tremendous inward-pushing pressure must generate all the heat and light that warms and brightens our world—and the rest of the solar system.

When an object is hotter than the surrounding material, the heat radiates away from the object. Then the object cools and contracts, which produces more heat, causing the process to continue. Physicists calculated that, in the case of the Sun, the process would continue for a very long time—about 100 million years. Based on these findings, the conversion of gravitational energy into heat seemed like a good explanation for the Sun's radiance.

However, scientists soon discovered that Earth, the Sun, and the planets have been around a lot longer than 100 million years. As you learned earlier, our solar system formed approximately 4.6 billion years ago. Scientists couldn't think of any process that would generate heat continuously for that long! In fact, no one came up with a satisfactory new theory for many, many years.

Before the pieces could fall into place, scientists had to do some serious physics. They had to gain a better understanding of atoms, develop the theory of relativity, invent *quantum mechanics*, and prove that the Sun is mostly hydrogen. All these discoveries began to build on one another in rapid succession at the beginning of the twentieth century.

Solving the Sun's Puzzle

In 1926, Sir Arthur Eddington put the first piece of the puzzle in place. He based his work on Einstein's famous equation $e = mc^2$. In this equation, e stands for energy, m stands for mass, and c stands for a constant—the speed of light, which is always the same. Since light travels very fast—186,282 miles (299,792 km) per second—this equation shows that a very small amount of mass is required to create enormous energy.

Eddington looked at the atomic weights of hydrogen and helium and surmised that four hydrogen atoms might combine to form one helium atom, with a loss of atomic weight of 0.7 percent. His idea, now known as nuclear fusion, was nothing more than a hunch, but if he was right, the small weight loss could account for an enormous energy release. Eddington calculated that if the mass of the Sun were pure hydrogen, it could continually produce energy for 10 billion years. Now, the time span fit what geologists already knew about the age of Earth.

Sir Arthur Eddington, a British astronomer, was the first person to suggest that a process now known as nuclear fusion might be taking place deep within the Sun.

However, Eddington had not quite proved his point yet. Did the Sun have enough hydrogen to fuel this process for as long as he had estimated? Physicist Cecilia Payne-Gaposchkin (1900–1979) cleared up this part of the problem by showing that hydrogen is the main ingredient of all stars.

Cecilia's Insight: The Stuff the Sun Is Made Of

Cecilia Payne-Gaposchkin was born in England in 1900, but moved to the United States to attend Radcliffe College in Boston, Massachusetts. In 1925, she became the first person ever to receive a Ph.D. in astronomy from that prestigious school. To earn her degree, she wrote a paper reflecting her thinking and research on the composition of the atmosphere of stars. At the time, astronomers were unsure about some strange results they had obtained when looking at the spectrograms of stars. There seemed to be a lot of unexplained variation. Most scientists believed that the variations represented differences in the amount of elements found in different stars.

Payne-Gaposchkin argued that the variations actually reflected differences in the temperature of stars. She also suggested that stars are composed primarily of hydrogen and helium. It took other astronomers some time to accept Payne-Gaposchkin's ideas, but they finally realized that she was right.

Always in love with the excitement of science, Cecilia Payne-Gaposchkin once remarked, "The reward of the young scientist is the emotional thrill of being the first person in the history of the world to see something or to understand something." To her, science was its own reward. Always modest, she once said her success was "a case of survival, not of the fittest, but of the most doggedly persistent."

In 1934, Cecilia Payne-Gaposchkin (right) received an award for outstanding work in the field of astronomy.

Hydrogen in the Sun

We now know that hydrogen is the most common element in the universe, so it's no big surprise that the Sun contains a lot of it. What may be more surprising is that there's comparatively little hydrogen on Earth.

Hydrogen is the lightest of all the elements. Huge, massive objects in space have plenty of gravitational pull, so they can easily trap hydrogen. The four planets known as the gas giants—Jupiter, Saturn, Uranus, and Neptune—are all massive enough to hold large quantities

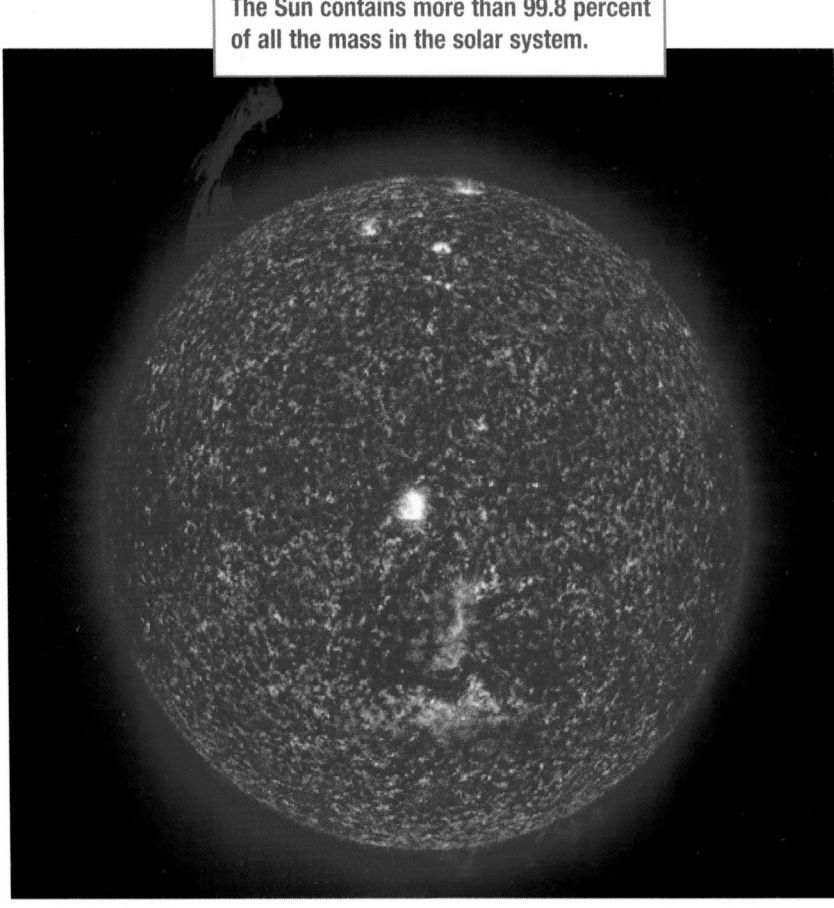

The Sun contains more than 99.8 percent of all the mass in the solar system.

of hydrogen. However, hydrogen easily escapes from lightweight objects in space because they do not have strong gravitational fields.

The Sun is huge. In fact, it is ten times larger than Jupiter—the largest planet in the solar system. If you rolled all the planets in the solar system up in a single ball, you would have to put together 1,000 such balls to equal the Sun's mass.

The Sun attracts so much hydrogen that as the layers of gas are pulled inward by the star's tremendous gravity, they crush the Sun's core. As you have just learned, all the heat and pressure at the Sun's center causes nuclear fusion. Nuclear fusion is sometimes compared to the explosion of a hydrogen bomb—and the release of energy is comparable. However, all a bomb's energy is released in a single moment, while energy from nuclear fusion is released steadily over a long period of time.

Nuclear Fusion: A Closer Look

Nuclear fusion begins when hydrogen atoms are stripped of their single electron, leaving behind a proton. In this way, the neutral atom is transformed into a positive ion. This single proton, moving randomly among other protons jumbled together in the core, goes through a tediously long process of banging into other protons and repelling them, and then colliding again, over and over. Because all these particles have the same positive charge, they don't naturally attract one another, so they keep on moving and crashing into each other.

Meanwhile, gravity continues to pull material in, the Sun's core continues to contract, pressure continues to build, and the core gets hotter and hotter. As the core heats up, the protons move faster and faster. Eventually, the protons are moving so fast that they overcome the natural tendency of positively charged particles to repel one another.

A single proton typically flies around inside the Sun for about a million years before it is moving fast enough to fuse with other protons, but when it hits that critical point, watch out! As soon as two protons fuse, one of the protons immediately gives off energy and becomes a

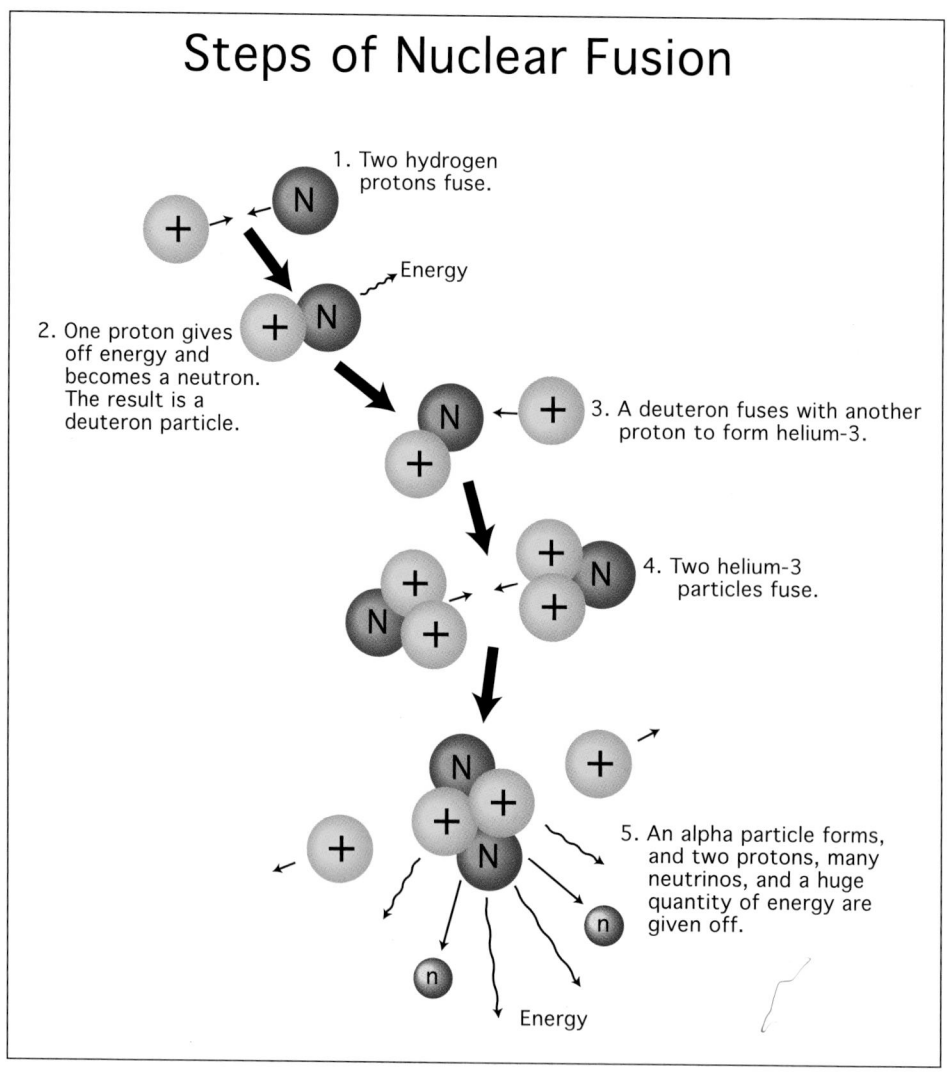

Steps of Nuclear Fusion

1. Two hydrogen protons fuse.

Energy

2. One proton gives off energy and becomes a neutron. The result is a deuteron particle.

3. A deuteron fuses with another proton to form helium-3.

4. Two helium-3 particles fuse.

5. An alpha particle forms, and two protons, many neutrinos, and a huge quantity of energy are given off.

Energy

neutron. The result is a particle called a *deuteron*—a nucleus formed by a proton and a neutron. However, this combination is very unstable, and the deuteron instantly combines with another proton, forming a particle called helium-3—a nucleus with two protons and a neutron.

Then the helium-3 nucleus combines with another helium-3 nucleus to form helium-4, which is better known as an *alpha particle.* An alpha particle is composed of helium's usual two-proton nucleus and two additional neutrons. It is a very stable structure. The two extra protons from the two helium-3 nuclei are ejected, and so is a tremendous amount of energy and some tiny particles called *neutrinos.*

So if nuclear fusion takes so long to get going, how can the Sun keep us warm day after day? How does the nuclear powerhouse keep going? The Sun burns bright all the time because there are so many protons in the Sun's core. While one proton is still a million years away from fusion, many others are on the threshold of nuclear fusion at any given moment.

Because all the particles produced during nuclear fusion have long-term stability, it is no surprise that humans have always considered the Sun to be a reliable, predictable source of energy. Unaware of the many violent and chaotic aspects of the Sun's activity, people simply basked in the sunlight that found its way to Earth.

The Case of the Missing Neutrinos

Even after physicists figured out how the Sun produces energy, one nagging question still left them scratching their heads. Based on their new understanding of nuclear fusion, scientists knew that the Sun must release vast quantities of tiny neutrinos—particles so small they

Wolfgang Pauli predicted the existence of particles that we now call neutrinos.

can pass through almost any substance without leaving a trace. They are ghostlike, invisible, and nearly impossible to detect.

No one had ever observed neutrinos when physicist Wolfgang Pauli predicted their existence in 1930. At that time, atomic theory was just a few decades old. Physicists had shown that atoms are usually electrically balanced, and they knew that the atoms of each element have a specific number of protons and electrons. For example, hydrogen has one proton and one electron. Theorists quickly realized that other tiny particles were also involved, and they developed methods for detecting most of these particles so that they could observe their behavior.

When Pauli saw that the calculations for nuclear fusion did not quite work out, he reasoned that tiny, invisible particles with no electrical charge must be created during nuclear fusion. A colleague, physicist Enrico Fermi, proposed the name "neutrino" for these mysterious particles. The name means "tiny neutral one." Although most scientists accepted the idea of neutrinos, no one could detect them.

Neutrinos are so small that when one passes through Earth, there is only a 1-in-200-million chance of its colliding or otherwise interacting with any matter. As one physicist remarked, "They sail through space, through walls, through planets, never even slowing down. Every minute, trillions of solar neutrinos flit through our bodies at nearly the speed of light." For two decades, everything physicists knew about this

In addition to naming the neutrino, Enrico Fermi made other substantial contributions to the development of atomic theory

tiny particle was based completely on theory. Then, finally, in 1956 a neutrino was detected!

Many mysteries about neutrinos remain, though. Scientists have only been able to detect between one-third and one-half the number expected from a nuclear fusion source. Developing techniques for detecting neutrinos is important because if scientists can get an accurate count of the number of neutrinos streaming from the Sun's core, they should be able to precisely calculate the rate of nuclear fusion within the Sun.

So what happens to all the neutrinos that scientists hypothesize are streaming from the Sun, but can't detect? Where are the missing neutrinos? Scientists have no answers to these questions. Perhaps the neutrinos change form during their long journey to Earth.

Researchers would also like to know whether neutrinos have mass. If they do, neutrinos may account for what scientists call "the missing mass." According to current theories about the formation of the universe, there should be more mass in space than astrophysicists have found so far. In fact, theorists estimate that about 90 percent of the mass in the universe remains undetected! Could neutrinos account for this tremendous discrepancy between the universe's theoretical mass and what scientists have been able to quantify?

Chapter 5

The Sun's Layers

Scientists can't actually see inside the Sun, but they have developed a variety of ingenious methods for detecting what goes on there. As a result, we now know that the Sun's interior contains layer upon layer of brilliant radiation, seething heat, highly agitated vertical movement, and powerful magnetic fields.

Much of what researchers know about the Sun's deep interior is based on comparisons and calculations. Using what they have learned from basic Earth-based experiments that look at how heat is generated and how it radiates, or flows, scientists study what takes place on the surface of the Sun. From surface observations, they have calculated the Sun's mass and measured its level of energy output, or luminosity, in a

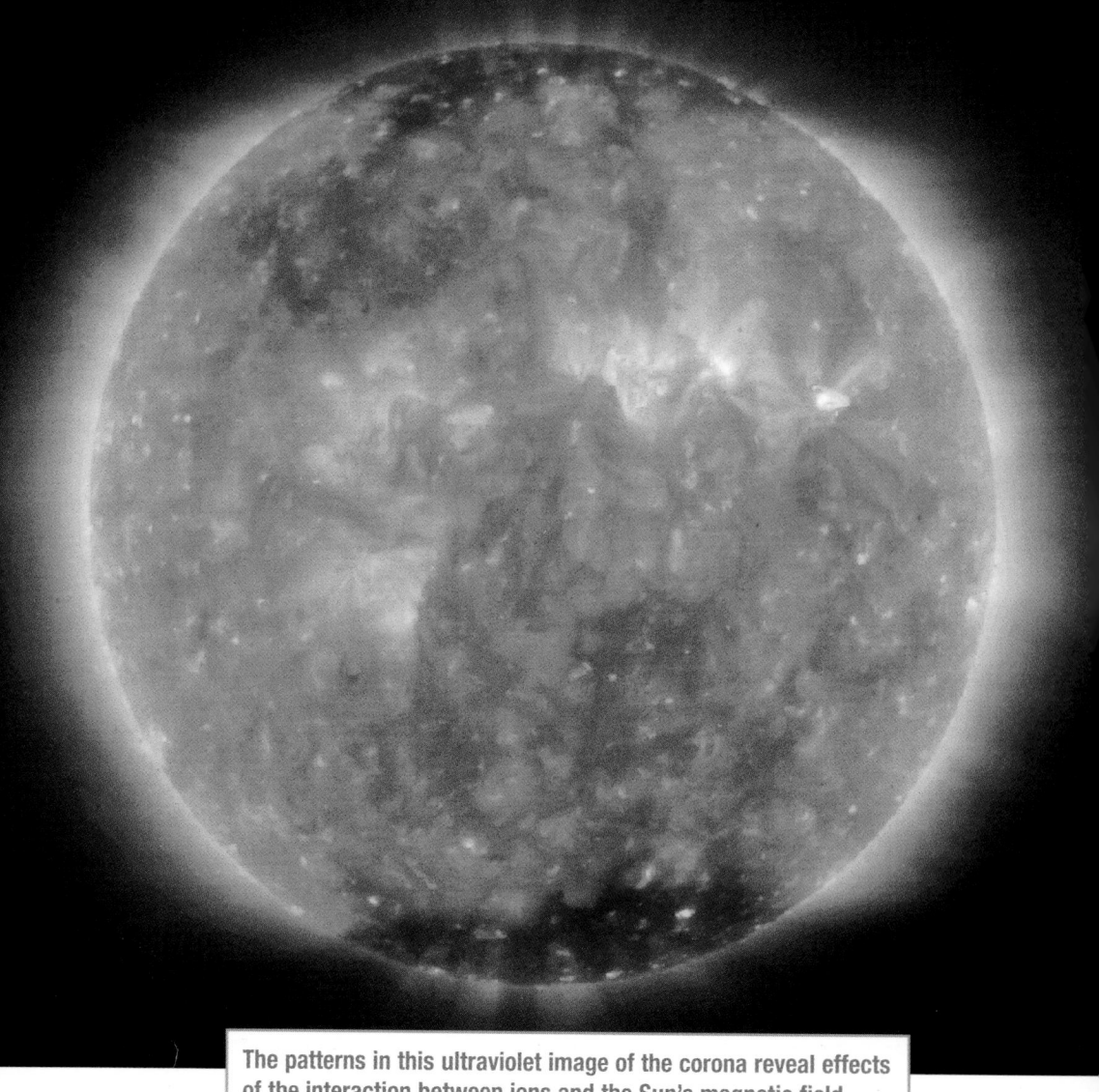

The patterns in this ultraviolet image of the corona reveal effects of the interaction between ions and the Sun's magnetic field.

given period of time. Using this information, scientists have then been able to deduce what goes on inside the Sun—probably with a high degree of accuracy.

The Sun's Inner Layers

The Sun's core accounts for only about 1.6 percent of its total volume, and it extends about 25 percent of the total distance from the star's center to its surface. Yet, the core's mass makes up about 50 percent of the total mass of the Sun. As you learned earlier, this massive energy-producing center is surrounded by two spherical layers—an inner radiative zone and an outer convective zone.

The radiative zone lies just above the core, and its gases radiate heat outward from the core. The radiative zone is under such tremendous pressure and exposed to such unimaginably high temperatures that the gases trapped there cannot move around or bubble upward.

Radiation cannot speed through this region either. It zigzags, bouncing off the upper boundary, zipping back down into the interior, bumping, ricocheting, and diffusing over and over. It gets reabsorbed, then radiated again, then deflected, then rerouted. Its path is random and reckless—a lot like a bumper car at a crowded carnival. Following a single particle from the core to the outer boundary of the radiative zone would take 170,000 years.

The convective zone is wrapped around the radiative zone like the peel around an orange. Because this zone is farther from the core, the gases there are cooler than those in the underlying radiative zone. At these lower temperatures, the outflow of radiation slows to a relatively sluggish pace.

When heat moves into the convective zone, the gases in this region expand, become lighter, and float upward toward the Sun's surface. As they move closer to the coldness of space, the gases cool, condense, grow denser, and sink back through the convective zone to the regions near the radiative zone. There, they become reheated and begin their journey again. The full round trip takes about 10 days. Ultimately, though, they escape through the transition region at the convective zone's outer edge, and make their way into the photosphere.

Scientists investigating the Sun have used information from the spacecraft *SOHO* to learn more about the unseen interior. They have become keenly aware that the convective zone is an active place. Scientists have also learned that all that activity causes the overlying photosphere to heave up and down like a boiling mudpot at Yellowstone National Park—but on a cosmic scale. The photosphere's heaving can raise the Sun's visible surface a distance of 6 to 19 miles (10 to 30 km), and may move it 10 feet (3 meters) or more per second horizontally. By studying these movements, scientists have found ways to understand some of the mechanisms that go on deep within the Sun.

Using data gathered by *SOHO*, researchers have discovered that the photosphere's heaving is caused by sounds that are trapped within the Sun and course throughout the interior. Human ears will never hear these sounds, though—they are too low in frequency, and they cannot travel through the vacuum of space.

Hot gases churning within the convective zone produce the sounds. The noise travels upward toward the surface and attempts to escape from the Sun's interior, but the photosphere reflects it back inward. As the sound waves bounce off the photosphere and rebound, they affect the photosphere's gases. The gases rise and fall in response to the bombardment. The movement is slow and rhythmic, repeating its pattern about once every 5 minutes.

Researchers estimate that some 10 million vibrating regions produce the notes, or sounds, that make up the Sun's "song." Each sound corresponds to a specific vibrating region. To understand the complex code, researchers must identify the source of a particular pitch. Then, by measuring the speed at which the sound is traveling, they can identify the variances of temperature, density, and composition through which the sound has traveled. In this way, scientists can create a fairly accurate model of the Sun's interior.

Through a telescope, the photosphere—the outermost visible layer of the Sun—shows evidence of the powerful *convection* process that goes on inside the sun. Images taken at high magnification show tiny, bright areas called *granules* that are surrounded by darker areas. These are the tops of convection cells.

These cells may look small from Earth, but in reality they are huge—about 620 miles (1,000 km) across. They are several hundred miles wide, and extend downward several hundred miles into the convective zone. Heat rushes upward through these tunnels toward the lower boundary of the photosphere. Then the gases cool off, grow darker, and fall back into the Sun's interior. Like bubbles in a pot of boiling water, these cells carry heat to the surface and then bounce it back down to start over, again and again. Meanwhile, the photosphere captures energy radiated by the convective zone and emits the light you see every day.

The Sun's Outer Layers

Some of the Sun's most magnificent displays take place in its transparent outer layers, or "atmosphere." As you have already learned, vast, looping jets and bridges of hot plasma shoot out from the corona. In

Loops of very hot, highly ionized atoms, or plasma, burst from active areas on the solar surface. These loops, which follow the lines of the Sun's powerful magnetic fields, reach temperatures as high as 1,800,032°F (1 million°C).

these regions, you can see signs of the turbulent and violent processes that take place deep within the Sun, and then burst into view.

The Sun's gases cool considerably once they enter the photosphere. At the innermost boundary of the photosphere, temperatures start out at a sizzling 12,140°F (6,727°C). By the time gases travel the 186-mile (300-km) thickness of the photosphere to reach the chromosphere, they have cooled to about 7,600°F (4,200°C). That's a big difference for two sides of a relatively thin layer.

In the regions above the photosphere, the enormous eruptions and belchings of the chromosphere and corona make powerful sunspots seem mild by comparison. Here, huge explosions rock the Sun many times a day. Some of these explosions are 400 billion times more powerful than the atomic bomb that destroyed much of Hiroshima, Japan, in 1945. As you learned earlier, these upper layers also interact with the Sun's magnetic fields to generate flares, prominences, and coronal mass ejections (CMEs).

The chromosphere's sparse, nearly invisible gases were first spotted by observers during a solar eclipse. These gases usually become visible just before or after the totality phase of a solar eclipse. At these times, the chromosphere appears as a thin red, rose, or pink outline around the edges of the Moon.

The chromosphere is a transition region between the underlying photosphere and the overlying corona. Gases moving from the photosphere to the chromosphere form clustered jets of hot gas, called *spicules,* that spike upward in short spurts.

As the Sun's gases move farther and farther from the intense heat and pressure at the Sun's central core, you would probably expect them

The **TRACE** satellite took this image of violent activity in the Sun's transition region—a thin thermal layer between the chromosphere and the corona.

to cool down, but, in fact, they heat up. Strangely, the chromosphere's temperature is actually higher at its outer edge than in its lower regions. As you would expect, the lower zone of the chromosphere is cooler than the underlying photosphere—about 7,600°F (4,200°C). Then, as the gases move away from the photosphere toward the icy regions of space, the temperature rises dramatically. At the outer border of the chromosphere, temperatures spike as high as 17,540°F (9727°C).

Amazingly, the gases in the corona—the outermost layer of the Sun—are even hotter than those in the chromosphere. Even ancient astronomers knew the Sun had a halo of bright light that extended far beyond the shining ball of gas we normally see. During a total solar eclipse, they could see these layers by looking at a reflected image of the Sun.

When the Moon completely blocks out the disk of the Sun, delicate brushes of white glowing light fan out from the Sun's poles and reach millions of miles into space. At the same time, long wide streamers of light extend from the region surrounding the Sun's equator. The corona's light is just barely visible as it juts out from behind the edges of the Moon's dark disk. Until the Sun's disk is blocked from view, though, the thin gases of the corona are always "drowned out" by the brightness of the Sun.

Today, scientists don't have to wait for a solar eclipse to view the corona. They can use a special instrument called a *coronagraph* to photograph the corona. This device was designed to block the Sun's disk from view on film—just as the Moon blocks the Sun's disk during an eclipse.

This total eclipse of the Sun seen from Baja, Mexico, reveals the white, glowing light of the Sun's far-reaching corona.

A coronagraph does not work well on Earth because the planet's thick atmosphere diffuses images of the corona.* It can, however, produce "eclipses on demand" when carried onboard a spacecraft and used from space, where Earth's atmosphere doesn't interfere. Natural solar eclipses last only a few minutes, and they may occur at times and in regions of the world that are inconvenient for observers. Coronagraph

---

* A coronagraph can, however, take outstanding photos of the chromosphere and its hot, glowing gases from Earth.

images can be taken at any time, and they make it much easier for scientists to study the corona.

Even though the corona is the Sun's outermost layer, its temperatures reach a sizzling 1.8 million°F (1 million°C). It is much hotter than the chromosphere or the photosphere. For a long time, this seemed strange to scientists. They wondered why the Sun's outermost gases were not cooler than its underlying layers. After all, the corona is hundreds of thousands of miles away from the nuclear furnace of the core.

Scientists have spent many years trying to solve this mystery, and in recent years, two robotic spacecraft have offered additional clues. When the spacecraft *SOHO* made observations of ultraviolet radiation from the Sun, the results surprised scientists. Even during the "slow," less active season of the Sun's 11-year cycle of activity, scientists saw that the corona is a vigorous, even violent place.

Additional data came from highly detailed images taken by NASA's TRACE spacecraft. These images show that the gases begin to heat up when they are in the region of the chromosphere that lies just above the Sun's visible surface. From this region, huge fountains of electrified gas shoot up, creating enormous arches of exceedingly hot gases. Millions of these sizzling-hot looping arches, called *giant coronal loops*, make up the corona. The loops may be up to 300 times hotter than the gases that make up the photosphere.

Scientists think most of the heating must occur at the base of the loops, within about 10,000 miles (16,100 km) of the photosphere's outer edge. As gas leaves the Sun's surface, it heats up and flows along the solar magnetic field, often soaring into huge arches wide enough

Giant coronal loops form the corona's tremendous halo of eerie light. Some scientists think these loops are caused by clashing magnetic fields.

to leap over an object more than 300,000 miles (482,803 km) high and thirty times wider than Earth. As the hot gases reach far out into space, they begin to cool and fall back toward the solar surface.

This new information helps, but one important question remains: What makes the gas heat up in the first place? No one knows the answer to this question.

In 1997, *SOHO* discovered that a carpet of magnetic field bundles covers the Sun's photosphere. From there, the magnetic fields loop up through the chromosphere and into the corona. These bundles are composed of pairs of field lines flowing in opposite directions. About once every 40 hours, two of these opposing lines merge and destroy each other. When they do, an enormous amount of energy is released. Some scientists think this process may be responsible for heating up the gases in the chromosphere and corona.

Solar Wind

In 1950, scientists suggested that the position of a comet's tail might be influenced by particles streaming away from the Sun, like a wind. Finally, in 1962, scientists developed a way to detect this solar wind. Of course, solar wind is not really a "wind" because it is not made up of moving air. After all, there is no air in the vacuum of space. Instead,

The thin white lines in this illustration represent the solar wind as it carries the Sun's magnetic storms toward Earth. The force of the solar wind shapes Earth's protective magnetosphere (the blue lines surrounding Earth) and interacts with it, creating beautiful aurorae and causing electrical disruptions.

The Flying Comet Tail

Sometime in the past, you may have seen a comet cruising across the night sky. Up close, a comet is like a dirty snowball made of rock and ice. Most comets travel around the Sun in an extremely long, *eccentric orbit*. Their journey extends beyond the planets to a region of space known as the Oort Cloud.

Named after Dutch astronomer Jan Hendrik Oort, this cloud is thought to be the birthplace of comets, which are made up of materials left over from the formation of the solar system. Disturbances in space occasionally jolt a comet loose from its orbit in the Oort Cloud and send it hurtling toward the Sun.

As the comet zooms through the inner solar system, the Sun's heat begins to melt the comet's ice. The ice transforms into a bright gas that surrounds the comet's central nucleus and streaks out to form a long tail. As the comet moves toward the Sun, its tail extends toward the outer solar system. After the comet circles the Sun and heads back to the Oort Cloud, a strange thing happens. Its tail continues to "point" toward the outer edges of the solar system. Now the tail is leading, rather than following, the comet's main body. What could make that happen? The solar wind is responsible.

Comet Hale-Bopp as it streaks across the sky above moonlit Zion Canyon, Utah.

solar wind consists of particles that flow through space at very high speeds.

In 1969, scientists began to understand the source of solar wind. First they discovered holes in the corona. Next, they realized that steady streams of high-speed particles continuously rush through these holes—escaping from the Sun and invading the far reaches of the solar system.

The interaction of the solar wind and Earth's magnetic field produces the Van Allen radiation belts, two donut-shaped regions containing energetically charged particles. The first of these is about 4,000 miles (6,437 km) above Earth's surface, and the second is about 8,000 to 12,000 miles (12,875 to 19,312 km) from the surface.

As you learned earlier, solar wind fluctuates over time and is sometimes further disrupted by CMEs. When the ionized particles associated with a CME crash into our planet's magnetosphere, dramatic magnetic storms often result. On a clear night, especially in far northern or far southern regions of Earth, you can sometimes see aurorae—stunningly beautiful evidence of storms raging within the magnetosphere.

The shimmering colored lights of the aurora borealis hang like a great curtain above an evergreen forest near Fairbanks, Alaska.

As you look up into the darkness of night, a strange reddish glow appears on the horizon. The red patch grows until you see gauzy streamers of color arcing overhead. The colors shimmer and shift. They glow green, then white. The colored lights hang in the sky like a massive curtain lit by spotlights. In the north, this display goes by the name of aurora borealis, or the northern lights. In the south, it is called the aurora australis, or southern lights. In either case, it is one of nature's truly dazzling and awesome displays.

Solar Disturbances on Earth

The interaction of charged particles in the magnetosphere does more than produce beautiful displays of light. It can also interfere with power lines, cause power outages, and knock satellite electronics out of operation. As Earth's technological human society becomes more dependent on computers, telecommunication, the Global Positioning System satellites, satellite news and weather feeds, and traffic lights, these outages become more serious. In 1989, solar disturbances interrupted electrical service throughout Canada's province of Quebec—an area covering 595,000 square miles (1.5 million sq km).

Chapter 6

When the Sun Dies

The Sun has used up a little less than half its fuel—so it is clear that its light and heat will not last forever. But don't worry. Enough fuel is still left to keep the Sun going for several billion more years—most experts estimate at least 5.4 to 7 billion years. Its death will not affect even your great-great-great-great-grandchildren or any of their close descendants.

However, the time will come when the Sun uses up all the hydrogen in its core. That moment will begin the final stage of our star's evolution. The Sun will begin to release nuclear energy at a vastly slower rate, and the energy balance maintained within the Sun for billions of years will end. The core will contract and become even hotter.

When this happens, the Sun will jump-start with a new series of nuclear reactions. But this time, helium, which used to be the product, will become the fuel. Like hydrogen, helium can also undergo fusion—but only at much higher temperatures. While hydrogen's fusion point is 18 million°F (10 million°C), helium requires a sizzling 180 million°F (100 million°C). When this happens, the Sun's outer layers will swell, then cool. The star will slowly become a *red giant*—a relatively cool, very large, and highly luminous star. At this point, the Sun's atmosphere will probably extend beyond Earth.

If the Sun does not get hot enough to begin fueling fusion with helium, its outer layers will expand more slowly. As they do, they will become cooler and brighter. By 6.5 billion years from now, the Sun may be a huge, swelling orange disk at least 3.3 times its present size. Either way, the heat will boil away Earth's

Aldeberan, also known as the Bull's Eye, is a red giant star in the constellation Taurus.

oceans and destroy its atmosphere. Eventually, the Sun will expand even more—up to 100 times its present size. Its atmosphere will extend outward into the solar system, surrounding both Mercury and Venus.

In old age, the Sun will continue to collapse, becoming hotter and hotter and denser and denser. What was once a great and mighty Sun will shrink to a star about the size of Earth—puny and silent compared to its notorious past as a sassy star with a violent streak. Finally the Sun will become so dense that it can no longer contract any further. At that point, the Sun will become a *white dwarf* and emit a white-hot glow.

In the end, the last of the Sun's glow will dim and then go out. It will finally become what astronomers call a *black dwarf*—a cold, dark, lifeless cinder. The remaining planets and their moons will no longer be visible in the frigid blackness that surrounds the Sun, but they will continue to follow their lonely orbits in the dark.

White dwarf stars are hot, compact, and very dense.

This fate, however, is billions and billions of years in the future. Long, long before the Sun dies, humans will have had the chance to make changes. It is very likely that humans, or their descendants, will have found a way to leave Earth in search of a new home.

Scientists and science-fiction writers have explored this subject for years and many agree that we face many challenges in the centuries and millennia to come. So far, scientists have not found any other spot in the universe that could support humans for an extended period of time. As a result, some scientists have begun to refer to our planet as "rare Earth."

We will also have to learn much more about space travel and about the regions of space beyond our solar system. Nevertheless, many opti-

This photo of Earthrise taken by Apollo 8 astronauts from the Moon made us realize how small, beautiful, and fragile our planet is.

mists agree that—as long as we can take good care of our planet and each other—our descendants will have most or all of the answers to these questions by the time the Sun begins to wane. Then somewhere, in another corner of the universe, a new colony of humans—or their descendants—may become established and grow.

Missions to the Sun

Vital Statistics

Spacecraft	Kind of Mission	Year of Launch	Sponsor
Pioneer 5	Solar orbiter	1960	NASA
Pioneer 6	Solar orbiter	1965	NASA
Pioneer 7	Solar orbiter	1966	NASA
Pioneer 8	Solar orbiter	1967	NASA
Pioneer 9	Solar orbiter	1968	NASA
Skylab	Space station/solar observatory; orbiter	1973	NASA
Explorer 49	Lunar orbiter, solar observer	1973	NASA
Helios 1	Solar orbiter	1974	NASA/West Germany
Helios 2	Solar orbiter	1976	NASA/West Germany
Solar Maximum Mission (SMM)	Earth orbiter	1980	NASA
Ulysses	South-north solar orbiter	1990	NASA/ESA
Yohkoh	Earth orbiter	1991	Japan, United States, and Great Britain

Spacecraft	Kind of Mission	Year of Launch	Sponsor
SOLAR AND HELIOSPHERIC OBSERVATORY (SOHO)	"Halo orbit"; orbiter at a stable point between Earth and Sun	1995	NASA/ESA
ADVANCED COMPOSITION EXPLORER (ACE)	"Halo orbit"; orbiter at a stable point between Earth and Sun	1997	NASA
TRANSITION REGION AND CORONAL EXPLORER (TRACE)	Solar orbiter	1998	NASA
HIGH ENERGY SOLAR SPECTROSCOPIC IMAGER (HESSI)	Earth orbiter	2001	NASA

Exploring the Sun: A Timeline

1611 — Italian astronomer Galileo Galilei observes sunspots and the Sun's rotation.

1684 — The French Academy of Sciences establishes the size of the Sun and its distance from Earth.

1814 — Joseph von Fraunhofer observes dark lines in the spectrum cast by solar light.

1836 — Francis Baily discovers "Baily's beads" during an eclipse of the Sun.

1859 — Gustav Kirchhoff and Robert Bunsen show the significance of Fraunhofer's lines and establish the composition of the Sun as primarily hydrogen.

1889 — George Ellery Hale invents the spectroheliograph.

1907 — Albert Einstein first publishes his equation $e = mc^2$.

1908 — Hale discovers that sunspots have strong magnetic fields.

1939 — Hans Bethe figures out the role of nuclear fusion in the production of solar energy.

1960	— *Pioneer 5* solar monitor is launched into solar orbit.
1962	— Solar wind is first detected.
1965	— *Pioneer 6* solar probe is launched.
1966	— *Pioneer 7* solar probe is launched.
1967	— *Pioneer 8* solar probe is launched.
1968	— *Pioneer 9* solar probe is launched.
1969	— Observation of holes in the Sun's corona reveals the source of solar wind.
1973	— *Skylab,* the first U.S. space station, is launched. Between 1973 and 1974, it is staffed by three crews for a total of 171 days. Astronauts onboard take more than 150,000 images of the Sun.
	— The United States launches the *Explorer 49* solar probe to examine solar physics from orbit around the Moon.
1974	— *Helios 1* solar probe is launched by the United States and West Germany and is inserted into solar orbit.

1976 — *Helios 2* solar probe is launched by the United States and West Germany. Its orbit comes within 26.7 million miles (43 million km) of the Sun.

1980 — The *Solar Maximum Mission* (*Solar Max*) is launched by the United States to study the Sun during the active part of the solar cycle.

1984 — *Solar Max* is retrieved by Space Shuttle astronauts for repairs.

1990 — *Ulysses* spacecraft is launched by the United States and the European Space Agency (ESA) to study polar regions of the Sun.

1991 — *Yohkoh* solar probe is launched by Japan, the United States, and Great Britain to study high-energy radiation from solar flares.

1994 — *Ulysses* makes its first pass by the south pole of the Sun.

1995 — *Solar and Heliospheric Observatory (SOHO)*, a NASA/ESA mission to the Sun, is launched by ESA.

— *Ulysses* makes its first pass by the north pole of the Sun.

1997 — *Advanced Composition Explorer (ACE)* is launched by the United States into an orbit about 932,000 miles (1.5 million km) from Earth to observe galaxies, the solar wind, and the Sun.

1998 — *Transition Region and Coronal Explorer (TRACE)* is launched by the United States to study the upper atmosphere of the Sun.

1999 — *TRACE* begins its mission.

Glossary

alpha particle—also known as helium-4; the particle that forms when two helium-3 particles combine and two protons are lost

asteroid—a piece of rocky debris left over from the formation of the solar system. Most asteroids orbit the Sun in a belt between Mars and Jupiter.

aurora—a display of light caused by interaction between charged particles and a planet's magnetic field

black dwarf—a cold, small, dense, and dark star at the end of its evolution, when it has completely exhausted its fuel

chromosphere—a thin region of the Sun between the corona and the photosphere

comet—a small ball of rock and ice that usually travels toward the sun in a long orbit that originates on the remote outer edge of the solar system

convection—the rapid movement of gases or liquids as a result of a difference in temperature. Heat generally causes a gas or liquid to expand, becoming less dense, so the fluid rises. Cold causes a gas or liquid to condense and become denser and heavier, so it falls or moves downward.

convective zone—the layer of the Sun's interior that lies above the radiative zone and below the photosphere

core—the hot center of the Sun where nuclear reactions produce enormous quantities of energy

corona—the Sun's outermost layer; a massive region of hot, luminous gases extending far out from the Sun

coronagraph—a device that blocks out most of the Sun so that the sun's corona can be photographed

coronal mass ejection (CME)—a huge bubble of coronal gas that passes through regions of strong magnetic fields

deuteron—a nucleus formed by a proton and a neutron

$e = mc^2$—Albert Einstein's most famous equation. It states that energy (e) is equivalent to mass (m) times the speed of light squared. The speed of light is a constant (c)—186,282 miles (299,792 km) per second.

eccentric orbit—a highly elliptical, flattened orbit

electromagnetic radiation—one or more of a range of waves and frequencies of energy that make up the electromagnetic spectrum.

Radar and infrared rays are at one end of the spectrum and have very long wavelengths. Visible light is about in the middle. At the other end of the spectrum are types of radiation with such short wavelengths that they are invisible to humans, including ultraviolet waves, X rays, and gamma rays. The frequency of radio waves ranges from about 10 kilohertz to 300,000 megahertz and can be heard by humans.

giant coronal loop—one of the sizzling-hot looping arches that make up the Sun's corona

granule—one of many relatively small-scale convection cells in the photosphere where hot, upward-flowing gases are surrounded by cooler, downward-flowing gases

gravitational field—the region around an object that is affected by its gravitational pull

gravity assist—a maneuver in which a spacecraft circles a body in space and uses the object's gravitational pull to increase its acceleration

greenhouse effect—a natural warming process that occurs around a planet when heat from the Sun is absorbed by carbon dioxide in the atmosphere and remains trapped on the planet

ion—a charged particle; an atom that has lost or gained an electron

magnetic field—the area surrounding a magnet that is affected by the magnet's attractive force. Some planets have magnetic properties and, therefore, have a magnetic field.

magnetic field line—one of the lines along which a magnetic field has the greatest influence

magnetosphere—the vast area around a planet that is filled with electrically charged particles and electromagnetic radiation; it is caused by the interaction of the planet's magnetic field and the solar wind

matter—any substance that takes up space

nebula—a primitive cloud of gases and dust from which the Sun and the planets were born

neutrino—a tiny subatomic particle with no mass and no charge. It is released during nuclear fusion.

nuclear fusion—a process that takes place in the core of the Sun and other stars, releasing enormous energy when two atoms of hydrogen combine to form helium

nucleus—the central portion of an atom that is composed of protons and neutrons

penumbra—the light-colored area around the edges of a sunspot

photosphere—the "surface" of the Sun; the area of the Sun that we see

plasma—a highly ionized gas that contains nearly equal quantities of positively and negatively charged particles

quantum mechanics—a theory of the structure and behavior of atoms and molecules. It states that energy takes the shape of minute packets, known as quanta.

radiative zone—the layer of the Sun's interior that lies above the core and below the convective zone

red giant—a relatively cool, very large and highly luminous star

solar eclipse—a phenomenon in which the shadow of the Moon falls across Earth's surface as the Moon passes in front of the Sun

solar flare—a sudden eruption of hydrogen gas on the surface of the Sun

solar prominence—a mass of ionized gas that bursts into the corona and is influenced by sunspots

solar wind—a stream of highly magnetic particles that flows at high speeds from the Sun's surface

spectroheliograph—a device used to analyze the Sun's composition

spectroscope—a device used to determine what an object in space is composed of by examining the spectrum it emits

spicule—a column, or clustered jet, of glowing gases in the photosphere

sunspot—a dark spot that appears on the surface of the Sun

ultraviolet ray—the kind of radiation with wavelengths just shorter than those associated with visible light

umbra—the dark region at the center of a sunspot

white dwarf—an old star that is often white, usually very dense, small, and faint

To Find Out More

The news from space changes fast, so it's always a good idea to check the copyright date on books, CD-ROMs, and videotapes to make sure that you are getting up-to-date information. One good place to look for current information from NASA is U.S. government depository libraries. There are several in each state.

Books

Campbell, Ann Jeanette. *The New York Public Library Amazing Space: A Book of Answers for Kids.* New York: Wiley, 1997.

Estalella, Robert, and Marcel Socias. *Our Star—The Sun.* Hauppauge, NY: Barron's Educational Series, 1993.

Gallant, Roy A. *When the Sun Dies.* New York: Marshall Cavendish, 1998.

Gardner, Robert. *Science Project Ideas about the Sun.* Springfield, NJ: Enslow, 1997.

Hartmann, William K. and Don Miller. *The Grand Tour: A Traveler's Guide to the Solar System.* New York: Workman, 1993.

Kosek, Jane Kelly. *What's Inside the Sun?* New York: Rosen, 1999.

Sorensen, Lynda. *Sun.* Vero Beach, FL: Rourke, 1993.

Vogt, Gregory L. *The Solar System Facts and Exploration.* Scientific American Sourcebooks. New York: Twenty-First Century Books, 1995.

CD-ROM

Beyond Planet Earth, Discovery Channel School, P.O. Box 970, Oxon Hill, MD 20750-0970.
An interactive journey to the planets, including the Sun. Includes video footage and more than 200 still photographs.

Video Tape

Discover Magazine: Solar System, Discovery Channel School, P.O. Box 970, Oxon Hill, MD 20750-0970

Organizations and Online Sites

These organizations and online sites are good sources of information about the Sun and the rest of the solar system. Many of the online sites listed below are NASA sites, with links to many other interesting sources of information about the solar system. You can also sign up to receive NASA news on many subjects via e-mail.

Astronomical Society of the Pacific
http://www.aspsky.org/
390 Ashton Avenue
San Francisco, CA 94112

The Astronomy Café

http://www2.ari.net/home/odenwald/cafe.html

This site answers questions and offers news and articles relating to astronomy and space. It is maintained by astronomer and NASA scientist Sten Odenwald.

NASA Ask a Space Scientist

http://image.gsfc.nasa.gov/poetry/ask/askmag.html#list

Take a look at the Interactive Page where NASA scientists answer your questions about astronomy, space, and space missions. The site also has access to archives and fact sheets.

NASA Newsroom

http://www.nasa.gov/newsinfo/newsroom.html

This site features NASA's latest press releases, status reports, and fact sheets. It includes a news archive with past reports and a search button for the NASA Web site. You can even sign up for e-mail versions of all NASA press releases.

The Nine Planets: A Multimedia Tour of the Solar System

http://www.seds.org/nineplanet/nineplanets/nineplanets.html

This site has excellent material on the planets, including the Sun. It was created and is maintained by the Students for the Exploration and Development of Space, University of Arizona.

Planetary Missions
http://nssdc.gsfc.nasa.gov/planetary/projects.html
At this site, you'll find NASA links to all their current and past missions. It's a one-stop shopping center to a wealth of information.

The Planetary Society
http://www.planetary.org/
65 North Catalina Avenue
Pasadena, CA 91106-2301

Sky Online
http://www.skypub.com
This is the Web site for *Sky and Telescope* magazine and other publications of Sky Publishing Corporation. You'll find a good weekly news section on general space and astronomy news. The site also has tips for amateur astronomers as well as a nice selection of links. A list of science museums, planetariums, and astronomy clubs organized by state can help you locate nearby places to visit.

Solar and Heliospheric Observatory (SOHO) Mission
http://sohowww.nascom.nasa.gov/
This is the official site of the SOHO mission, a joint ESA/NASA mission to study the Sun's internal structure.

Ulysses Mission

http://ulysses.jpl.nasa.gov/

This is the official NASA site for information concerning the Ulysses mission and its discoveries.

Welcome to the Planets

http://pds.jpl.nasa.gov/planets/

This tour of the solar system has lots of pictures and information. The site was created and is maintained by the California Institute of Technology for NASA/Jet Propulsion Laboratory.

Windows to the Universe

http://windows.ivv.nasa.gov/

This NASA site, developed by the University of Michigan, includes sections on "Our Planet," "Our Solar System," "Space Missions," and "Kids' Space." Choose from presentation levels of beginner, intermediate, or advanced.

Places to Visit

Check the Internet (*www.skypub.com* is a good place to start), your local visitor's center, or phone directory for planetariums and science museums near you. Here are a few suggestions:

Exploratorium
3601 Lyon Street
San Francisco, CA 94123
http://www.exploratorium.edu/
You'll find internationally acclaimed interactive science exhibits, including astronomy subjects.

National Air and Space Museum
7th and Independence Ave., S.W.
Washington, DC 20560
http://www.nasm.edu/NASMDOCS/VISIT/
This museum, located on the National Mall west of the Capitol building, has all kinds of interesting exhibits.

Index

About the Authors

Ray Spangenburg and **Kit Moser** write together about science and technology. This husband-and-wife writing team has written 38 books and more than 100 articles. Their works include a five-book series on the history of science and a series on space exploration and astronomy. Their writing has taken them on some great adventures. They have flown on NASA's Kuiper Airborne Observatory (a large airplane carrying a telescope). They have also visited the Deep Space Network in the Mojave Desert, where signals from spacecraft are collected. They have even flown in zero gravity on an experimental NASA flight. Ray and Kit live and write in Carmichael, California, with their two dogs, Mencken (a Sharpei mix) and F. Scott Fitz (a Boston Terrier).